AWAKE UNTO RIGHTEOUSNESS

Righteousness is a precise biblical rev<

manity. My friend, Claudia Baca-Moor

a generation. Her superb book, simpli

Claudia for over 2 decades and apprec.. ... ..ve and service for His Kingdom. Not only has she and her husband, Wyatt, made a difference in the life of many in the Nations, but through their church, Glorybound, they have made a great difference in the city of Albuquerque, New Mexico. Claudia's gift as a teacher of the Word is very evident. Her anointing allows her to be easily understood by anybody whose heart is open to learn the truth. For that reason, I wholeheartedly endorse her book, *Awake Unto Righteousness*.

—MEL TARI
AUTHOR: *LIKE A MIGHTY WIND*

AWAKE UNTO RIGHTEOUSNESS IS SOLID! Claudia is an amazing combination of deep revelation and solid scripture-based teaching. This is made readily aware in her book, Awake Unto Righteousness. My favorite "Claudia Quote" from the book is, *"If you've done something and you feel you deserve to feel guilty, then you're paying a price that Jesus has already paid."* She has a marvelous gift to connect with people's hearts and brilliantly uses humor to either drive her point home or just to have a laugh! Claudia understands the reality of the struggles that people live with and offers a clear and powerful message of comfort and hope.

—HEATHER CLARK
LEAD WORSHIPER, CHRISTIAN PERFORMER AND EXHORTER

AWAKE UNTO RIGHTEOUSNESS; A "MUST READ" FOR EVERY BELIEVER!
Claudia Baca-Moore is an outstanding teacher with a special sensitivity to the Holy Spirit and a proven leader within the body of Christ. Her messages are always fresh and unique; leaving you hungry for more. I know you will be inspired by what she has to say in her latest book, *Awake Unto Righteousness*. Claudia's anointed ministry is marked by a joyful exuberance and a strong faith that knows how to take hold of God. Now take hold of this book; it is a "must read" for every believer!

—PASTOR STEVEN BROOKS
STEVEN BROOKS INTERNATIONAL ONLINE CHURCH, PUBLISHED AUTHOR AND ITINERANT SPEAKER

Awake unto RIGHTEOUSNESS

God is Greater than Your Guilt, Condemnation & Shame

CLAUDIA BACA-MOORE

Most ENCOUNTERS PRESS products are available at special quantity discounts for bulk purchase, sales promotions, premiums, fund-raising and educational needs. For details, please email: Publisher@EncountersPress.com or call: (918) 995-2177.

Awake Unto Righteousness by Claudia Baca-Moore
Published by Encounters Press, Tulsa, Oklahoma
Inspiring Hearts, Transforming Souls; One Book at a Time
Tulsa, Oklahoma, U.S.A.
Printed in the U.S.A.

Also by Claudia Baca-Moore:
• *Awake Unto Righteousness*
  Learn how God is so much Greater than Your Guilt, Condemnation and Shame.
• *Revelations from Heaven*
  Discover more beautiful facets of our Father God. There is so much more to Him than what traditional religion has portrayed. He unveils His mysteries to those who seek Him out.

Visit the Author's website at: **www.AuthorClaudiaBacaMoore.com**
Cover Design by: Encounters Press Design Team

While the author has made every effort to provide accurate Internet addresses at the time of publication, neither the Publisher nor the Author assumes any responsibility for error or for changes that occur after publication.

As publishers we want to be responsive to the issues that genuinely touch people's lives. One of our primary missions is to publish genuine human experiences, which reflect *authentic encounters with God;* tragedy to triumph, underdog victories and conquests over the impossible. Conjointly, Encounters Press' teaching and evangelistic books, provides church leaders, ministers and believers with biblical materials that will assist them in their individual missions. ENCOUNTERS PRESS will equip people with the truth of God's Word by *Inspiring Hearts & Transforming Souls; One Book at a Time.*

For a **FREE CATALOG of resources** from Encounters Press, please contact your Christian supplier or email us at: **Info@EncountersPress.com.**

I dedicate this book to my parents, Eric and Jessica Baca, who are now in heaven.

CONTENTS

◆ ◆ ◆

Why I Wrote this Book

When I was a very young Christian, the Lord spoke to me that I would be given a revelation for the End Times. I was thrilled. I thought of all the disasters and sufferings I had heard of concerning the End Times, and now I thought I was going to somehow be part of alerting the world to these calamities and help others be prepared. But that was not what I was given. Instead, the Lord shared with me a free gift He wanted all mankind to receive. Through the Blood of Jesus, Mankind would now have right standing with Him. Instead of shame, guilt, and condemnation, instead of Sin Consciousness, mankind could come before the God of the whole world and receive help.

This was very good news—first to me, because I was striving (unsuccessfully) to be perfect and holy before God by myself—and especially to the world, for Righteousness is a gift given by Jesus to all who would receive it.

It changed my life and exceeded my wildest expectations. What a revelation to share with a world that feels without hope, and to Christians who feel like they can never be good enough. I believe that you can't give away anything to another person that you don't first believe and possess in your own heart.

That is why I am writing this book. I believe I am Righteous—and so you can be also. I want to reach out to people as God has reached out to me, and let them know that God is your Father and you can talk to Him anytime, no matter what your own heart tells you. He is greater than your heart and welcomes you into His Presence. This Righteousness is not something you can earn, but you receive it when you come to Jesus. It is yours right now.

You have a *new nature,* a new DNA, like a *butterfly*—totally transformed. Nothing resembling that old caterpillar nature exists anymore. The *fresh* and *new* have already come. As you read this book, it is my deepest and fondest desire that you awaken to who you really are. ❧

Claudia Baca-Moore

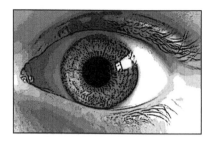

awake
[uh-weyk]

awoke or awaked or awoken, awaking.

1. to wake up; rouse from sleep:
I abruptly awoke at six with a deep sense of empowerment!

2. to rouse to action; become active:
His lacking interest awoke.

3. to come or bring to an awareness; become cognizant to:
She awoke to the realities of righteousness.

4. waking; not sleeping.

5. vigilant; alert:

◆ ◆ ◆

A Journey Toward Righteousness

s a Bible teacher, I always assumed that I knew a lot about righteousness. In fact, when God began to teach me specifically about righteousness, I was in my prayer closet. Early one morning as I was praying, He asked me, "What do you know about righteousness?" Of course, I said, "I know all about it!" Then I reeled off a list of ten or more scriptures about righteousness to Him. God said, "But what do you know about righteousness?"

Now, believe me, I know what the Word of God says. But the truth is, we can know a lot about what the Word of God says, but it doesn't do any good unless the Word of God "gets inside" us. That's when the Word becomes alive and full of power. Words written on a page, or our comprehension of what the scriptures say, doesn't necessarily make them alive and full of power. But when the Word gets inside us, it becomes alive. It becomes powerful. It will revolutionize our lives!

If I were to sit down with you and share the most important message I knew, I would tell you what Jesus Christ has done for us, and especially, what He has made us to be. He's made us one with his nature—and His nature *is* righteousness.

PART I

◆ ◆ ◆

Guilt

Guilt is cancer. Guilt will confine you, torture you,
destroy you as a person. It's a black hole.
It's a thief.

— Dave Grohl —

FEELINGS OF GUILT

In our pastoral ministry, we do a lot of counseling. Through years of listening to people, I've realized that most Christians are attacked by feelings of guilt. Even though Jesus died for our guilt—even though righteousness is the absolute opposite of guilt—most believers struggle with feelings of guilt from time to time.

Let's look into the Word of God to see what guilt does to us. The Word tells us that we are the righteousness of God in Christ.

But if we don't understand the opposing force to righteousness, we really don't enter into a full realization of its power. Let me give you an example.

We were at a Christian convention fairly recently when a man got up to preach and said, "Now, I know a lot of you deal with guilt . . ." That kind of caught me off-guard, because I truthfully wasn't feeling guilty about a thing at that moment. If you were my friend and you asked me, "What do you feel guilty about?" I'd say, "Honestly, I don't feel guilty about a thing. Whatever has happened in my past is past! There's nothing I can do about it." But this man kept pressing the issue, saying, "Something may have happened 10 years ago but you just feel guilty about it."

So I thought for awhile about things that had happened 10 years ago, 20 years ago, trying to remember something that I *might* be able to feel guilty about. Just so I could relate to what he was saying, I dredged up some stuff that I hadn't thought about in years. And, by the end of his teaching and prayer line (a prayer line to release your guilt), yes, guilt was all that I was feeling. Don't ever receive guilt, even under the best of pretenses. Don't even try to look back and think about what you did in your past that you could possibly feel guilty about. Why not? Guilt is from the devil—Let it go!

You say, "But you don't know all the bad things I've done, Claudia. The reason I feel guilt is because of the sinful things

I've done." Somehow we think the proper punishment from God for sinning is guilt. But I'll tell you something that you need to know—guilt is from the devil. It really is! Guilt is not the price that you have to pay for your wrong actions. I'll say it again—guilt is from the devil, and anything that is from the devil is something you don't need to have in your life.

Throughout the Book of Psalms, and elsewhere, people had the same struggles and the same difficulty with guilt. But in those days, all they had was the promise of what you and I have now in Jesus Christ. Psalm 31:10 says, *"For my life is spent with grief, and my years with sighing; my strength faileth because of mine iniquity, and my bones are consumed."*

I used to think that the word "iniquity" just meant "sin." I always wondered why the Bible would say, "for my sin and iniquity." If the word "iniquity" meant "sin," then why use both words in a scripture? After all, "iniquity" isn't really a very common word that we'd use in our everyday speech. There are certain Bible terms that we use, but that we don't really comprehend. The word "iniquity" can be easily translated with one word—guilt. So the Psalmist says, "Because of my guilt, this is what I've been feeling—I have grief, I have sighed, my strength is failed, and my bones are consumed." This is the "work" that guilt accomplishes in your life. It brings grief. I have never been drawn into a closer relationship with God during a time of feeling guilty. Feeling guilty has never strengthened me.

Guilt never produces anything beneficial in the life of a believer. But I have a friend who fell into sin of some sort, and her comment was, "I have to always remember what I did, and feel bad about what I did. That way, I'll never do it again." Guess what—she was wrong. According to the Word of God, she was sure to fall in to that same kind of sin again. Jesus' solution to a sin problem is really simple. If you see that you have committed a sinful action, ask God to forgive you—and He will. And according to the Word of God, we are to forget what lies behind, and to press on!

God wants us free from guilt. Regardless of its source, guilt is never something God will use to show you how to get out of sin. Guilt is condemnation, and condemnation is from the devil. Jesus died for that. Righteousness speaks, right? What does righteousness say? It says whatever God says. Whatever God says I am—I am, and I've got to stand in agreement with His opinion. We looked in the Word of God, and we saw that Jesus died spiritually. He became sin with our sin. He went to hell for us, and it was there that He defeated Satan and overthrew all principalities and powers. We've seen that righteousness produces something inside us. It's our state of being, and it produces righteous actions in our lives. Sure, there are a lot of people that do righteous acts. But, according to the Word of God, their righteous acts are as filthy rags unto God. The Word also talks about a people who went to produce their own righteousness, but they were ignorant about the whole subject. You and I need to know that we can't do anything on our own. It all depends on Him.

There was a cry in the hearts of mankind, saying, "God, I want to be in fellowship with you." The Old Testament book of Job addresses man's innate need for God. Job 25:4 asks, *"How then can a man be justified and righteous before God? How can he who is born of a woman be pure and clean? Behold, even the moon has no brightness compared to God's glory and the stars are not pure in His sight. How much less man who is a maggot* (isn't that a nice term?) *and the son of man who is a worm."* To paraphrase, he was saying, "You know, the sun, the moon—they're so huge, and the stars are so bright, but they're nothing in comparison with God. How can man, who is a worm, who is nothing—how can he ever be made righteous?" How can man ever be made clean? How can man, who was born into sin, ever be right before God? Jesus. Jesus!

Back to the writer of Psalms 31, "Because of my guilt I've had total grief. My strength fails," and then he says, "and even my *bones* are getting weak." This is what guilt will cause. It will cause you to be oppressed in your mind, it will make your heart feel terrible and it will start causing some physical manifestations in your body. Guilt will cause you to be weak. If it's from Satan, it's come to bring you down.

On to Psalms 38, verses 4-8: *"For mine iniquities are gone over my head; as an heavy burden they are too heavy for me. My wounds stink and are corrupt because of my foolishness. I am troubled; I am bowed down greatly; I go mourning all the day long. For my loins are filled with a loathsome disease, and there is no soundness in my flesh. I am feeble and sore broken: I have roared by reason of the disquietness of my heart."*

The Psalmist is talking about what guilt has done to him— it's so heavy that he's troubled, bowed down, and mourning all the day. There is no soundness in him. He's feeble, sore, broken and disquieted of heart. Does that sound like something God would want to bring upon us? Consider it as if you were a parent. If your children were doing wrong, you'd be sure to break them. That way, they're going to be real good—right? Make sure that they have such a heavy burden of guilt on them so they can't carry the load. That will help them straighten out—right? Wrong on both counts! Do you know what *will* happen? They will finally get so discouraged that he or she will just give up and say, "I can't do it. Why even bother trying?" That's what the Law does. The Law makes us see something that we can never live up to, and that, in turn, causes rebellion.

Psalms 40:12 says, *"For innumerable evils have encompassed me about. Mine iniquities have taken hold upon me so that I am not able to look up. They are more than the hairs of mine head; therefore my heart faileth me."*

This is more of what guilt feels like. The Psalmist says, "Guilt feels like it's so heavy I can't even look up." If you feel guilty, if you feel like you've done something wrong to somebody, exactly how eager are you to see that person? Hardly. If you allow yourself to feel like God is somehow holding something against you because of what you've done, what you've thought, or what you've felt—how quickly will you want to come boldly to His throne of grace? Not very! That's when we start reacting to God as if He were some sort of bill collector; collector of a bill that we could never pay.

You say, "But Claudia, when I do something wrong, I *do* feel guilt." That might be true—but *stop*! Don't allow it. In the same way you resist sin, resist guilt. Guilt is a consequence that Satan would like to impose as a result of sin, but our actions are none of his business—it's a matter that's between you and your Father. Resist guilt like you would resist sickness. Resist it like you would resist the devil himself, by standing on the Word of God. If you've done something and you feel you deserve to feel guilty, then you're paying a price that Jesus has already paid.

Just because you can read scripture and see the result of guilt, it doesn't mean that it's a Godly or God-desired result. In these cases, the effects of guilt have been just what Satan wants to see and do. Psalm 66:18, *"If I regard iniquity in my heart"*—remember regard means "to look to"—*"If I look to guilt in my heart, the Lord will not hear me."*

That's the thought, but then it goes on to say in the very next verse, *"But verily God hath heard me, He hath attended to the voice of my prayer."* Unrighteousness makes us feel like crying, "God, you can't hear me." Guilt makes us feel, "God, you have no way to listen to me." That's when we have to bring His Word to remembrance. We must remember that not only did God send Jesus to become our unrighteousness for us, Jesus became guilt for us. We understand that Jesus became sin for us, but we forget that one of the results—perhaps the main result—of sin is guilt. Designed to keep you broken and torn, to keep you weak, to keep you bowed down without even being able to look up. Now, if Jesus took our sin upon Him (which, of course, He did), He also took the results of sin upon Him. And one of the results of sin is guilt. In the same way that you know you've been set free from sin, you can know that you've been set free from guilt!

CONVICTION AND GUILT

I'm not going to bring "guilt scriptures" to your attention so you can improve your ability to feel guilty. Everybody usually does pretty well at that, without my help. I want to discuss these scriptures so that we can see the other side, the side that is absolutely the counterfeit. Most people think that "conviction" and "guilt" have meanings that are quite similar to one another. Not true! "Conviction" and "guilt" are not at all the same. Guilt says, "You did it, you blew it, you're rotten, you're terrible and you can never fix it. It will never work out." Whereas conviction says, "It happened, but it can be fixed. It happened, but walk close to the Lord and He'll make better than if it had never happened. He has a way of escape for you." You see, there's a *big* difference between conviction and guilt. They're not even in the same category!

Unfortunately, many well-meaning Christians who think that guilt and conviction are one-in-the-same receive guilt as though it's from God. They reason that, "I've blown it and I have to deal with the consequences. After all, I sinned, and I have to pay the price." Wait—*My* Bible says that *Jesus* paid the price. So why receive that "after all, it's my fault" stuff? "Oh, but Claudia, what if I have sinned willfully?" Then let God strengthen you. The blood of Jesus Christ not only forgives you of all sin but also continuously cleanses you of all sin and unrighteousness.

In the Gospel of John, chapter 16, Jesus was talking to His disciples about the Holy Spirit. He was saying, "Look, guys, I want you to know that, very soon, I'm going to go away from here." Put yourself in the disciples' place as they heard these words from their Master. They had given up their homes, they had given up their families, they had given up their business and they were following Jesus. Then, all-of-a-sudden, Jesus hits them with this bombshell. Naturally, their response was, "You can't go away from us, Jesus. Wherever you go, we'll go!" But Jesus was telling them something that was actually good news—they just didn't know it at the time. In John 16:7, Jesus says, *"Nevertheless I tell you the truth; It is expedient for you that I go away: for if I go not away, the Comforter will not come unto you; but if I depart, I will send him unto you."*

These next few verses are very important—*"And when he is come, he will reprove the world of sin, and of righteousness, and of judgment: Of sin, because they believe not on me; Of righteousness, because I go to my Father, and ye see me no more; Of judgment, because the prince of this world is judged,"* (John 16:8-11).

John says the Holy Spirit comes to convict the world about sin. He doesn't come to convict the world of their *sins*—notice that in John 16:9, there's no "s" at the end of the word "sin." The Holy Spirit doesn't come so that the world will know that they're in sin. The Holy Spirit comes to convict the world of only one sin—the sin of not believing in Jesus. Often, the "gospel" that is preached by the church is, "Hey world, stop having abortions. Hey, sinners, stop being homosexuals. Hey, world, you're perverse—stop it!" But that's not the gospel that Holy Spirit is talking about. Believe in Jesus. That's the gospel. That's what will change someone's life!

Now, I'm not trying to ask you a "trick question." But if I were to ask, "How many of you believe the Holy Spirit convicts us of sin?" Many of us would raise our hands. If I asked, "How many of you believe that the Holy Spirit comes and convicts *you personally* of sins in your life," most of us would say that we do. That's because we have heard it preached over and over and over again, "The Holy Spirit has come to convict us of sin." But that's not what the Word of God says in these verses. John says that the Holy Spirit comes to convict the world—not Christians, the world—of sin.

I've heard it preached all my Christian life, and I've probably said it many times myself, "The Holy Spirit convicts me of sin." But think of a person who you are in close fellowship with. It might be your husband, your wife, your best friend, whatever your closest personal relationship might be. What if that person's main job was to convict you of sin? What if they were always showing you what you were doing wrong? "I don't like the way you look today." "Couldn't you talk a little softer, a little louder?" If you had a friend like that, how long would you keep on being friends? If it were me, I wouldn't be friends with them very long at all. Scripture tells us that as we raise our children, we should raise them in the way they *should* go. However, most of us raise our children in the way they should *not* go. We tell our children, "Don't do this, stop doing that, quit doing this."

The Holy Spirit reacts in a similar way when there is sin in our lives. I'll tell you what He does *not* do. He doesn't say, "Look what you're doing. Why are you doing this? You're in sin. This is wrong. Don't do it. Quit it." When there's an action of sin in our life, He says, "Hey, you're not a slave anymore. You don't have to do this. You're not subject to sin, that's not your nature. If you'll awaken to your righteous nature, you won't sin."

The Holy Spirit does not convict the Christian about sin. Now, I know that statement may hurt your head a little bit, but it's scriptural. The Holy Spirit does not convict the believer of the *action* of sin. Rather, he shows us the way of escape every time!

God's concentration is not focused on what you and I are doing wrong. I don't care who tells you that it is! There's so much preaching on sin, on all the sinful things that we do, and on all the things that God is not pleased about. But God wants you to know that, as His child, He's very pleased with you. He's the One who says, *"For if our heart condemn us, God is greater than our heart, and knoweth all things,"* (1 John 3:20). God isn't interested in the *action* of sin. He's interested in you and me. He's interested in our hearts. But so many times, we think that God's main interest in us is to get us to stop doing wrong things. The Holy Spirit came to convict the world of one sin, and one sin only—that they did not believe in Jesus.

And, He didn't just come with a message to the world that said, "Hey, world, you're not believing in Jesus." His message goes on to say, "But there is righteousness available to you because Jesus has gone to the Father, and you see Him no more." The only way that righteousness could be offered to you and me outside of our actions is if it is given to us as a gift—an exchange, His nature for ours. Jesus became One with our sins, One with our unrighteousness, One with everything that we were. That way, we could be one with His righteousness. His nature could be imputed to us rather than having to be earned by us. He says, *"For the Son of man is come to seek and to save that which was lost,"* (Luke 19:10). Jesus would to return to the Father only after becoming the Supreme Sacrifice for the whole world. "And this is the thing I convict the world of also, that judgment has already happened and Satan has been condemned already and judged already" (paraphrased from John 16).

If Satan had not been judged and condemned already, guess who'd be in authority in this world—Satan would. But the Holy Spirit has come to tell the world, "You don't have to submit to his yoke of bondage. You don't have to be depressed and sick and hurting." The Christian should already know this truth and be living in it. But the world doesn't know. The Holy Spirit, through us, wants to bring this message to the world.

But we spend so much time trying to get *ourselves* out of sin. Some years ago, I belonged to a church that talked a lot about the "judgment of God." They'd counsel, "There are problems in your life, Claudia. God wants to judge those problems, and that's why you're under the judgment of God . . ." I submissively bought into it for a long time. They made me believe that God disapproved of my life, and that He was judging me. Now God may disapprove of my actions in certain situations, but God is not disapproving of me. The Bible teaches that, instead of judging us and pointing out faults, He took every bit of that judgment and wrath and poured it upon Jesus.

That's the difference between the Old Testament and the New Testament. In the Old Testament, His Word was a mirror for you and me to look in. It showed us all of our faults, and proved to us that we desperately needed a Savior. The New Testament is a mirror, too. But when we look into the mirror of the New Testament, we see the perfection of Christ in us. I look at His Word and see that I am love. I am peace. I am full of the fullness of God, and every ability that He has is mine. Never in the New Testament does the mirror of God's Word point out imperfection. According to God, there is no imperfection in the new creation. According to God, we've been made complete and we've been made perfect. We don't ever have to look in His Word, asking, "God, what sins do you need to convict me of today? God, what sins am I doing? What am I doing that's displeasing to you?" That's not relationship. If there are areas in your life that God wants to change, then He'll do it. Here's how: "Come here. Look, I've given you strength and ability. Come this way." He tells us what *to* do. He leads us. God is constantly wooing us, so that we can awaken unto the righteousness already within us.

In John 16:8, the Bible says, *"And when he is come, he will reprove the world of sin, and of righteousness, and of judgment."* Does every one of your Bible translations say "the world"? The definition of "world" here is "the ungodly multitude." How many of you belong to the ungodly multitude? "World" refers to men and women who are alienated from God, people who are hostile to the cause of Christ.

As believers, we are not "of the world" in that sense. We are not obstacles to the cause of Jesus. We are not alienated from God. That means, what the world is—we are not. Therefore, we conclude that when the scriptures talk about the Holy Spirit convicting "the world" of sin, He's not referring to you and me.

The Holy Spirit has already convicted me of sin—past tense. The Holy Spirit came and convicted me that Jesus came into the world. At first, I didn't believe it. The Holy Spirit continued to convict my heart, telling me that there was righteousness available to me because Jesus has gone to the Father. The Holy Spirit convicted my heart that Satan is nothing, and has no power over me. He showed me that Satan has nothing in common with me because of what Jesus has done. That Satan has been judged already.

The Holy Spirit is in fellowship with me. He's my friend, my encourager. When I was in grade school, I had some teachers that would always tell me, "You're not going to make it. We're going to have to hold you back." But my father always said, "Come on Claudia. You're younger than everyone else is, but you'll be able to do it." My father was the kind of person who was didn't always point out the things I was doing wrong. He would talk about the things that I was doing right, and what I could do to be right. Our Father God reacts the same way to us. He doesn't try to show us what we're doing wrong. If somebody "gets all over my back" about how I'm being, and points out all my wrongdoings, it doesn't motivate me to change. I have yet to have somebody tell me what a lousy, crude, horrible person I am, and make me think, "Wow, they're right. I want to change so badly." Concentration on wrongdoing only serves to bind a person into sin.

God would never say, "You're sick. You've got pain. There are all kinds of horrible things going on inside your body. You're in some real trouble," then leave it at that. Why? Because He's greater than any sickness or illness. He's the Healer, and He's confident of His healing power. It's the same way with sin. God doesn't come to reveal sin, because He's greater than sin—He's overcome the sin and deprived it of power, making sin ineffective in your life. He set you free! He doesn't want our concentration to be on sin, so why would His concentration be on sin? He doesn't want our concentration to be on works, so why do we think that His concentration is on works?

God sets His mind on the fresh and the new that is come. His concentration is on who we are in Christ and who Jesus is in us. *That's* who *we* are! He points us toward the Word of God.   He guides us toward the blessings of our inheritance. He's looking for us to convict the world, so they will believe in Jesus, and in righteousness, and in His judgment.

THE DEFINITION OF RIGHTEOUSNESS

Let's look at some definitions of "righteousness" as taken from several different dictionaries as well as from several well-known Christian authors, so that we are in agreement about the meaning of this very important word. Basically, I would say that righteousness is "to be made right." That's the simplest definition I have heard of the word "righteousness"—to be made right. What if you and I could, in our heart of hearts, really know that we've been made right? What if we knew that not all of our actions are a product of who we are, that some of our actions are a result of "old thinking" in some areas of our thought processes? What if we knew that in God's sight, He saw us as right? He saw as whole, all the time.

Another definition of righteousness says it is "to be made right, to be in a condition that's acceptable to God, to be in a state which man receives approval from God, to be innocent." Innocent—I love that word! I can assure you; one thing I *never* felt in my childhood was innocence. But when Jesus came into my life, He made me innocent. I like to meet people that have that kind of spiritual innocence about them. In God's sight, we believers truly are innocent through the Blood Sacrifice of His Son, Jesus. He says we wholly and absolutely possess the character and quality of being right or just.

"Righteousness" was translated into modern English from the old English words "right wiseness." It was used to describe the attitude of God, which demonstrates His righteousness, His faithfulness, His truthfulness. It referred to all that is consistent with His own nature and the promises of His Word. Right-wiseness was exhibited in the death of Christ, so God could give it as gracious gift to all men. That gift of righteousness is given to all who believe in Christ Jesus. We are brought into right relationship with Him. Righteousness is unattainable by obedience to any law, by any merit on man's own part, or by any condition other than faith in Christ. The man who trusts in Christ becomes the righteousness of God in Him, and he becomes all that Christ is. Righteousness fulfills all the requirements and expectations that God ever had regarding mankind. Man simply could not meet those requirements and expectations on his own!

E.W. Kenyon defines righteousness as, "the ability to stand before God without a sense of guilt or inferiority." As I explained above, the opposite of righteousness is guilt. Righteousness is the gift that God gave us in order to put us in right standing with Him. We couldn't have earned it—we couldn't have done it—but somehow we think that we can obtain righteousness by what we do, by our good works. Have you ever heard people say, "So-

and-so sinned, and now he's unrighteous"? We must understand that righteousness, as God speaks of it, is not an action, it's not what you do—it's who you are. It is a *state of being*.

No matter what I do, no matter what actions I perform, I cannot change the fact that I'm Mexican, or that I'm female. I could undergo a few surgical operations, I could put blue contact lenses in my eyes, and I can dye my hair blonde. I could change a lot of things about my outward appearance, but I can't change what I am on the inside. But when I got born again, my very nature changed. My old nature died, and my new nature is the righteous nature of Jesus Himself. Now, no matter what I do, regardless of my outward actions, that new nature cannot be taken from me.

In a marriage situation, just about every couple has an opportunity to argue and quarrel. Disagreements, tempers can rise up. But when these things happen, it doesn't end the marriage covenant. It doesn't annul the marriage vow. In a marriage, when you fight, it doesn't mean that you're divorced. You're just out of fellowship.

That's the way it is in our relationship with Christ Jesus. When we sin, we do not become unrighteous. We don't drop out of the kingdom of light and go back into the kingdom of darkness. In our thinking, we're out of fellowship with God. "Oh, no, Claudia," you say, "God can't look upon sin. If we have committed any sins, God can't look upon us." Well, then isn't it interesting that God says, *"Let us therefore come boldly unto the throne of grace, that we may obtain mercy, and find grace to help in time of need,"* (Hebrews 4:16).

If He can't look upon sin, how could anyone ever go before Him to get forgiveness? He can't look upon sin? Well, He can look upon me, because I'm not sin. When He looks upon me, He looks upon Jesus. I'm the very righteousness of God in Christ. That's why it is so very important that we understand this fact: we can never lose our righteousness. It's our state of being!

SIN CONSCIOUSNESS

Isaiah says, "When You and He make Him an offering for sin . . ." He is our offering for sin. Yes, God planned to redeem mankind from sin. That's why He said, "I've come to seek and to save. I have come so that I could give my life as a ransom for many," (paraphrased from Luke 19:10). How sad that Jesus came and fulfilled His mission, completed the sacrifice—and His people are still preoccupied with a sin problem! The Psalmist said, "When I regard sin in my heart, I cannot hear God," (Psalm 66:18). When you and I give place to sin in our hearts, we can't hear God's voice. God doesn't want us to be ever conscious of wrongdoing. God wants us to meditate on His power to make us right.

The more we talk about all the things we *shouldn't* do, the more we think about that very thing. It's not that we're rebellious—it's called "sin consciousness." God wants us to be "righteousness conscious" instead. He wants our concentration to be on all the things that Jesus did right in our behalf. He wants our concentration to be on who and what He has made us to be as new creations in Christ. I'm not righteous because of *my* works—I'm righteous because of *His* works. I wasn't such a wonderful person that God had to say, "Okay, I owe it by obligation to make you righteous." But Jesus did it for me!

Inescapably, we've all experienced the agony of sin-conscious at one time or another. Every one of us has experienced feeling guilt, shame, and thinking that we've been a disappointment to God. None of it has ever had its source from God's heart, but we have all experienced these feelings. Many times, leaders in the Body of Christ have taught us that this is how God views us. But remember—that's how Jesus felt when He was on the cross. He began to feel forsaken of God. He began to feel like a worm, a no man. He began to feel paranoid, that everyone was talking about Him. That's how unrighteousness feels. Jesus experienced all of that, so that you and I would never have to experience it.

But during those times when you *have* felt as though you're unrighteous, something very dangerous and destructive can happen. Sin-consciousness, guilt and condemnation make you to feel like you can't approach God. It causes us to feel like we are not deserving of the blessings of God, and that He would be perfectly just in withholding those blessings from us. It makes us feel like there's no way we can step out in faith and do anything for God, because there's obviously something that's not right in our lives.

Job 25:4-6 says, *How then can man be justified with God? Or how can he be clean that is born of a woman? Behold even to the moon, and it shineth not; yea, the stars are not pure in his sight. How much less man, that is a worm? And the son of man, which is a worm?"*

Job is crying out, saying, "Look, I have this sense of unrighteousness. I have this sense that I can never be right before God."

The Psalmist writes, *"If I regard iniquity in my heart, the Lord will not hear me,"* (from Psalm 66:18). Many Christians are so conscious of their iniquity, their sin, and all their wrong actions that they're not able to hear God. They don't believe that God hears them, either. That happens when a person meditates upon their actions and their wrongdoing, instead of focusing on their right being.

To "regard" means "to look, to focus on, and to make that what you are seeing." If you look and you focus on something, that's the direction you're going to go. Pastor Allen Speegle tells a story about a lonely road in his part of the country. The road has absolutely nothing on it. Just miles of straight, flat road, with nothing on either side—except for this one big one tree. One tree, and miles and miles of nothing else. But people say that, without fail, motorists run into that tree every week. It happens that for some reason, drivers start focusing in on that tree. When they do, they start driving in that direction, and pretty soon—BAM!

That's what happens when we regard iniquity and sin in our hearts. It causes us to focus in on a particular problem, and we can't see past it. Let's imagine that you have a flat tire. I pull over behind you and say, "Yep, it's a flat tire. Flatter than a flutter. You're not going anywhere—not for awhile, at least. You've got yourself quite a problem here! I'll tell you how you got that flat tire. You ran over a nail. You didn't have good enough tires. Your car's too old and dirty, and you were probably driving too fast, besides."

I could tell all about your problem, in great detail and with great accuracy. Does that help you? Does it help you get going again? You can tell somebody why their sin is wrong, and exactly what their problem is. You can get right to the root of it, but it still doesn't help. You've got to give them the answer. If you have a flat tire, you need a spare. That's the solution. If you have a sin problem, you need to receive God's righteousness!

Typically, we introduce the new believer into a form of sin-consciousness the minute we lead them to Christ. How? The traditional "sinner's prayer" does it. If somebody came up to you right now and said, "I want to receive Jesus," most Christians would lead him or her in "the sinner's prayer." It goes like this: "Father, forgive me of my sins. I believe that Jesus Christ died and rose again. I believe I'm forgiven. I receive Jesus as my Lord and Savior. Amen."

Now, parts of that prayer are wonderful, powerful, and lead to eternal life. But one element of that prayer, while sounding spiritual enough, isn't Scriptural. It can even be harmful to the thinking of the new convert!. Nowhere in the Word of God does it say that you have to have your sins forgiven in order to be born again. The Bible does say, *"Whosoever shall call upon the name of the Lord shall be saved,"* (Romans 10:13). It also says, *"If thou shalt confess with thy mouth the Lord Jesus, and shalt believe in thine heart that God hath raised Him from the dead, thou shalt be saved."* —Romans 10:9

So where did we get the "Father, forgive me of my sins" part? When a person confesses Jesus Christ as Lord, they are at that moment being transported out of the kingdom of darkness into the kingdom of light. The Word of God tells us that when we become a new creation, we die. The old man is dead. That person, as he was, doesn't exist anymore. So, whose sins are you asking forgiveness for—the old, spiritually dead man, or the new creation in Christ? It's a waste of time to ask God to forgive the sins of a person who no longer exists. It makes just as much sense as it would to perform heart surgery on a dead body!

Now, I know that probably 90% of all Christians came into the Kingdom of God having prayed a prayer very similar to the one I described. The reason it can be dangerous, not just unscriptural, is because it immediately introduces into a new kind of sin-consciousness. When we pray that prayer, saying, "Father, forgive me my sins," we think God's first priority is to get us to stop sinning. That is not God's first concern. God's main priority is *you*. So much so, that God made sure sin couldn't keep us from Him. That's why He sent Jesus—to take care of sin, to "destroy the works of the evil one," (1 John 3:8). When we begin relationship with God by saying, "Father, forgive me of sin," every time from that day forward we think that God is looking for us to do wrong. ❧

PART II

◆ ◆ ◆

Righteousness

For He made Him who knew no sin to be sin for us, that we might become the righteousness of God in Him.

— 2 Corinthians 5:21 —

THE ANSWER: RIGHTEOUSNESS

But if a sense of unrighteousness can cause all of that, shouldn't a sense of righteousness bring an opposite result? That's why we need to concentrate on making an awareness of our righteousness an important part of our unshakable foundation in the Gospel of Jesus Christ. Abraham was given promises from God, and we're told that Abraham made those promises his own. Abraham said, "Yeah, that's for me," and he made it his own.

Think about it this way. A number of people hear that each of them has won $100,000. Now there'll be some in that group who won't believe it when they hear it. There'll be others in the group who'll say, "You're kidding me! I've got $100,000? Yeah, sure," and then not do anything about it. But there'll be some in that group who'll say, "All right, $100,000! Where is it? I want it! I'm going to make it mine!"

Enough about that $100,000—let's get back to righteousness. We can't be among those who don't believe the truth. Nor should we be numbered with those who acknowledge the truth, but who do nothing about it. We must understand the truth about our righteousness in Christ, and walk in the freedom that it gives to us.

God made a way through Jesus Christ for us to be made righteous outside of our works. Keep this in mind—He who knew no sin became sin so that I could become the righteousness of God in Christ. He did not *do* sin, He *became*. Similarly, I don't *do* righteousness, I've *become* righteous. Therefore, I act out of my nature. Jesus did not commit a sin to become sin—He just became. We do not commit a righteous act to become righteous. We just become! It's a gift. We didn't earn it; we could never earn it.

THE GIFT OF RIGHTEOUSNESS

When the preacher stands in the pulpit and says, "Today we're going to preach on holiness," they're usually saying, "Today we're going to preach on what you don't do right. We're going to preach on the things you need to get right so God will be pleased with you." Aren't you glad that we're learning that righteousness, holiness, and right standing with God means so much more? Righteousness is the very nature of God. It is what makes God who He is. God is perfect, and His nature is righteous. That same righteousness has come as a free gift to whosoever would receive Jesus Christ. We have been given righteousness, which is the very nature of God Himself.

The concept of "gift" is something we need to talk about. Sometimes it's difficult to understand the goodness of God's love for us, or that His righteous nature has been given to us as a gift. Remember, one does not earn a gift. We have a right to go before God as though we had *never ever* sinned. Our sins weren't just covered over, or ignored. According to the Word of God, not only have our sins have been completely removed from us, the *nature* of sin has been removed from us. And we didn't earn a bit of it by our actions!

That's a hard truth to grasp, especially for the modern church. She has developed an accelerated consciousness of sin because of what has been preached time and time again for many decades. We've been told about all the things that God is displeased with. Thankfully, God is not as sin-conscious as the church has been. God isn't looking for you and I to do wrong, so that He can call us down on it. God wants us to awaken unto who we are. *"Awake to righteousness and sin not,"* says 1 Corinthians 15:34. God wants us to understand our new nature. God wants us to understand who we are!

We can never lose that which we have been born again unto. We can never lose our righteous state of being—it is a gift that's been given to us. I didn't earn it. I didn't obtain it by something I did in the first place, so how could it be taken away from me for something I did? Now, if somehow I had earned it, if my actions had gotten me my righteousness, then by my actions it could be taken away from me. But my actions never got me my righteousness—Jesus got me my righteousness!

Since I am not subject to the Law any longer, I'm not under the curse of the Law. It's very important for us to understand that righteousness is a gift. Righteousness is the element of my being which has made me acceptable to God. Righteousness has recreated me in His very own nature. Man could not give to himself, or remake himself in God's nature. If man could have done that on his own, Jesus wouldn't have had to come. That's why Jesus did come, and pay a price so that I could have His righteous nature as a free gift. And because this new nature was given to me as a gift, it can never be taken from me—no matter what I have done or might do. I didn't earn it, so it can never be taken from me on the basis of merit. Jesus is one who was absolutely righteous, and made us absolutely righteous in Him.

We must gain a more complete understanding of the new nature that's resident inside us. It's not enough to say, "I am the righteousness of God in Christ." We have to understand the blessings which that new nature has brought to us. We have to understand the great goodness of the gift. In Romans 1:16, Paul says, *"I'm not ashamed of the gospel of Christ, for it is the power of God unto salvation . . ."* A very familiar verse to most Christians. But then he says, *"For therein is the righteousness of God revealed from faith to faith, as it is written: the just shall live by faith."* —Romans 1:16-17

I'll read it to you another way. It says, "This is the Good News. This Bible tells us that God makes us ready for heaven, makes us right in His sight. When we put our faith and our trust in Christ to save us, this is accomplished from the start to finish by faith." As the scripture says, the man who finds life will find it through trusting God.

I don't know why so many believers seem to enjoy standing against the joy and peace of their Christian brothers and sisters. They tell you why you can't be joyful, why you can't be peaceful, and why you're absolutely not righteous. They'll be more than happy to tell you all the different reasons why you should be miserable. But don't worry about that. Just get *strong* in the Word of God. As we talk about righteousness, I don't want you to receive it as merely a truth or a principle in the Word of God. I want you to make it your own, to make it a part of you. I want you to see it as absolutely yours. George Bernard Shaw said, "Beware of false knowledge; it is more dangerous than ignorance." Do not allow the false knowledge and ignorance of others discredit and scorn your newfound revelation of righteousness! Make it yours!

THE RIGHTEOUS NATURE

We must understand the difference between "righteous actions" and "righteous being." There have always been miscon-
ceptions and misunderstandings about the difference between
man's actions and his state of being. Consequently, we have used
the Bible—God's Word sent to build us up and to show us who
we were in Christ—to beat people down. The Bible is incorrectly
used to show man how far short he falls concerning the things of
God. What God wants is that His Word be used to show us how
much He has brought us in unto Himself! God does not want
His Word to be used as a sword that slices people into pieces—he
wants His Word to be used as a tool, which would build us up in
our inheritance as Sons. Correctly divined, His Word shows us
that we are just as righteous as Jesus is.

Romans 3:21-25a says, *"But now the righteousness of God without the law is manifested, being witnessed by the law and the prophets;
even the righteousness of God which is by faith of Jesus Christ, unto
all and upon all that believe. For there is no difference: For all have
sinned and come short of the glory of God; Being justified freely by His
grace through the redemption that is in Christ Jesus: Whom God hath
set forward to be a propitiation through faith in His blood, to declare
his righteousness for the remission of sins that are past, through the
forbearance of God."*

This demonstrates God's righteousness. In His divine forbearance, He had passed over and ignored the former sins without punishment. He demonstrates and proves at the present time—in the "now"—that He Himself is righteous, and He justifies and accepts as righteous whoever has faith in Jesus. In order to be considered a righteous man in times past, you had to do righteous acts. But now God says, "A righteousness has been revealed that mankind has longed to see. It's a righteousness which exists outside of the law. This righteousness is not anything that man can earn, but—because I am gracious—anyone who would believe becomes just as righteous as **I Am**."

We'd better take a moment to discuss the meaning of the word "gift." It's a simple word with a clearly understood meaning. So, why is it, then, that while we know that God gave us the "gift" of righteousness, we don't *receive* it as a gift. A gift is something that is not earned—it's just given, with no thought or pretense of getting something in return. Furthermore, a gift is something which should never be taken back. A gift comes with no conditions, no strings attached. Imagine giving a gift to someone. Then, after not having seen them around for awhile, you'd say, "Give me back my gift. I don't like the way you've been. Give it back." Entirely permissible, right? Of course not—that's not a gift at all! If I required you to do something for that "gift," it then should be called a "wage." If I promised to give you something, but what I want you to do is this, do that, and then do some other things, then I'll give you this gift, it's not a gift, because I'm making you do something to obtain it.

It is as if we acknowledge that God has given us His gift of love, His gift of the Holy Spirit and His gift of righteousness. Then we worry about what we must do to earn those gifts. Worse yet, when we see that we fall short of earning those gifts, we think then He's going take them away! Never. He's the giver of good gifts, and a gift is something that is freely given by the bestower to us without ever expecting a return.

In the same way that guilt and condemnation keeps us from the presence of God, a sense of righteousness keeps us going deeper *into* His presence. In the same way that sin and guilt-consciousness keeps us from stepping out in the things of God, an awareness of our righteousness in Him causes us to step out; causes us to go forward. We are convinced that God is for us and not against us, so we make bold expeditions into the realm of faith.

The answer to the problem of sin, and sin consciousness, is righteousness. *"Awake unto righteousness and sin not"* it is not two separate commands. It is actually just one process of thought. If you came to my kitchen and said, "Claudia, I'm hungry," I could say, "Eat, and be hungry no more." I didn't give you two separate commands. I said, "Eat, and when you do, you're not going to be hungry anymore." Of course, we could instead draw out a chart, show you a videotape presentation of the human anatomy and inform you, "You're hungry because your digestive tract works like this . . . and you haven't eaten, which would cause your body to do this-and-that." But is it helping you? Or, is it making the problem worse? Absolutely! We need to give the answers to the problem, not add more problems to the problem. So, eat and be hungry no more. Awake unto righteousness. Put your focus on righteousness, not in iniquity, not on sin, not on guilt. Put your concentration on who we have become through Christ.

THE FRUIT OF RIGHTEOUSNESS

The Spirit of Righteousness was the very same Spirit that raised Christ from the dead. And that Spirit of Righteousness is the very same Spirit that quickens (heals) our bodies today. We were born again unto righteousness. Righteousness does not refer to our actions. It is our nature. In the same way that my physical nature is female, my spiritual nature is righteousness. That's who I am, that's who I've become. As a result, the Holy Spirit produces the "fruit of righteousness" in me.

Our righteous nature will produce righteous actions, but righteous actions could never produce a righteous nature in us. There are plenty of people in the world who perform righteous actions, or good works. So, they should go to heaven, right? They've been nice people, they've done good things. But the Bible says there's only one way to go to heaven, and that's to receive Jesus Christ as Lord and Savior. Consequently, there's only one way to not go to heaven—don't receive Jesus! As far as I know, there's only one sin God is concerned about, and that is the sin of rejecting of Jesus Christ. Our righteous actions are important for other people to see, but they're not important to God in regard to eternal life. Our nature is what's important to God. Who we are—who we've become through Christ Jesus—that's what is important to Him.

There is a power that is resident within you and me. We know that it has something to do with God the Father, God the Son, and God the Holy Spirit. And though Father, Son, and the Holy Spirit are righteous and they produce fruit, it is their *power* that produces the fruit.

John 15:5 says that Jesus is the Vine, and we're the branches. The branches aren't what which produces fruit—the fruit comes from the root, through the vine, then out onto the branches. As branches, we simply hold the fruit. That's the way it is with the fruit of righteousness. We don't have to go around, worrying, "I must produce fruit, I've got to have righteous fruit, I'd better get busy producing righteous fruit." I *am* righteous. Righteous fruit is produced by our righteous nature. It's something natural that is produced from God's inherent power within me.

Now, there may be some things that I write on these pages that you don't agree with, but we don't have to agree about everything, line by line. We can still walk in love. But you must always reserve the right to search out any doctrine or belief for yourself in the Word of God. Just because you've heard something taught and preached over and over again, it doesn't mean that it's scripturally correct. I looked up every scripture concerning sin in the Bible, and I found out something.

In Acts 2:38, Peter said to them, *"Repent, and be baptized every one of you in the name of Jesus Christ, for the remission of sins . . ."*

Wait a minute! He's saying, "I want you to know Jesus so that you can be released of and from sin." When Peter says, "repent," he's not saying, "stop sinning." The word "repent" simply means "to change your mind, to turn away from, and towards" something else. So, Peter is saying, "Change your mind and be converted, that your sins may be blotted out."

When Stephen was being stoned to death (at the end of the seventh chapter of Acts), he knelt down and cried with a loud voice, *"Lord, lay not this sin to their charge."* Just like Jesus at the cross, the words of the Holy Spirit in Stephen spoke about forgiveness of sin!

Here are a few more Bible verses which speak of how God deals with sin:

"For whosoever shall call upon the Name of the Lord shall be saved," (Romans 10:13).

"Be it known unto you therefore, men and brethren, that through this

man that is preached unto you the forgiveness of sins," (Acts 13:38).

"Blessed are they whose iniquities are forgiven, and whose sins are covered." (Romans 4:7).

"Blessed is the man who the Lord will not impute sin." (Romans 4:8).

"But the God commanded His love towards us, in that, while we were yet sinners, Christ died for us." (Romans 5:8).

"Knowing this, that our old man was crucified with Him, that the body of sin might be destroyed, that henceforth we should not serve sin. For he that is dead is freed from sin," (Romans 6:6-7).

"For in that He died, He died unto sin once: but in that He liveth, He liveth unto God. Likewise, reckon ye also yourselves to be dead indeed unto sin but alive unto God through Christ Jesus our Lord," (Romans 6:10-11).

"But God be thanked, that ye were the servants of sin, but ye have obeyed from the heart that form of doctrine which was delivered you. Being then made free from sin, ye became the servants of righteousness," (Romans 6:17-18).

I could go on—but, hopefully, I've made my point. When we examine what the scriptures say about sin, we find that Jesus conquered it. When we study what the scriptures say about the "old man," we learn that he died, he no longer lives. The "old man" is dead. When Jesus talked about sin, it was to say that we've been set free from it. And yet, how much emphasis does Christianity put on the action of sin? God cannot be pleased about this! We act as though the blood of Jesus wasn't as powerful as sin. There's only one sin that separates us from Him—the sin of not believing in Him. But you and I *do* believe in Jesus. Therefore, sin cannot separate us from Him. He has defeated sin, so we could have relationship with Him.

It's very important—no, it's *vital* in our Christian walk—that we understand that God's view of sin is that it's been defeated. If, indeed, that is God's view of sin, then what should your view of sin be? That it's defeated! No more thinking, "Sin is working in me, and any moment it could come out. You know, I'm subduing it right now but you don't know what evil lurks within me." Evil does not live within the new creation.

You and I don't have two different natures. We're not spiritually torn between being born again and not being born again. We don't posses the nature of the devil along with the nature of God. We're not partly in the kingdom of darkness, and partly in the kingdom of light. A person can have only one spiritual nature. We didn't have two natures before we believed in Jesus, did we? Well, we certainly don't have two spiritual natures now! We live now in the kingdom of light, transported out of the kingdom of darkness.

And, that new nature within us produces fruit. Romans 6:22 says, *"But now being made free from sin, and become servants to God, ye have your fruit unto holiness, and the end everlasting life."* We have our fruit in holiness. Remember that fruit is something that is not produced by you and me, but the Holy Spirit produces it. The fruit that the Holy Spirit and His presence within accomplishes is love, joy, peace, patience, kindness, goodness, gentleness, and self-control (Galatians 5:22-23). It's His presence within that accomplishes these things.

I have rewards because I received Jesus Christ. I have holiness, given to me by God. And our righteousness produces good. It brings results. Now, it's by grace and not by anything that we have done. But our righteousness does produce—for us and for others. Because I am a pastor, I don't get around to a lot of other churches on Sunday mornings. But I hear preachers, and I see ministers on television who often talk about righteousness and holiness. Sadly, they speak as if it were produced by actions we perform. It's seldom referred to as a state of being resulting from a gift God gives. But we know that righteousness is a gift, not something that is earned. Therefore, it stands to reason that we've been given the fruit—the results produced *by* the gift, if you will—that goes along with the gift.

And so what are the fruits of righteousness? II Corinthians 9:10 reads, *"Now he that ministereth seed to the sower both minister bread for your food, and multiply your seed sown, and increase the fruits of your righteousness."* The righteousness in our lives will literally produce goodness and kindness. What a relief to not have to say, "I've got to be good, I've got to be kind, I've got to be charitable. I must do it. I've got to show forth good works, or else!" By awakening unto who I am, good works are my natural response to situations.

I don't wake up in the morning and think, "I've got to be a woman today. Okay, Claudia—try to be a woman." I don't have to work at it. I am a woman! I don't have to put major concentration on who I am, I just do things that are natural to me. I'm not talking about being a stereotypical person, either. I simply am who I am, and it's natural for me to be me.

In the same way, when you woke up to this morning, your spiritual nature was a nature of righteousness. You nature doesn't change because of circumstances. You don't go to sleep one night righteous, then wake up unrighteous just because you had a horrible thought or dream. Once you have been born again by grace through faith into the kingdom, you cannot be unborn by your works. Your actions did not make you righteous, and your actions cannot make you unrighteous. It's easy for us to *feel* like our actions can affect our righteousness. But if that were true, the reverse would have to be true as well. And that would mean that it would be possible for our actions to make us righteousness.

A couple of folks came to my office one day and asked if they could sit down and talk to me. While I was finishing up some work at my computer, they were having a conversation with each other.

I heard one of them say, "Did you know so-and-so's going to hell?" The other said, "Why do you say that?" And he replied, "You didn't know this, but he smokes!"

I'm on my computer, so I can't say anything. But I remember typing, "Therefore, whoever does not smoke goes to Heaven," on my computer. Because, if smoking can send someone to hell, then not smoking obviously will get us into Heaven! My works will not get me into Heaven, or keep me out of Heaven, either. Believing in Jesus Christ, and what He did at Calvary, is what gets me into Heaven. And, I can trust Him to keep me until then!

If we'll stop being so works-oriented and trust that God has made us right with Him, we'll stop hounding everyone else around us about what they're doing wrong. When you and I receive grace and mercy from the Father, we can begin to walk in grace and mercy. It becomes so much easier to deal with people around us.

True or false—the church that preaches the strongest against sin seems to be the church that has more sin in it than anybody else. It's true—if I were to, week after week, preach a message to our congregation that says, "Such-and-such is what you're doing wrong. You've got a sin problem, and here it is . . ." If I were to continually preach that to our church, the message of sin-consciousness would be so strong in the people that they would act accordingly. Many so-called "holiness preachers" concentrate on works, and I've watched so many of them fall, one after another. But that's not the message Jesus preached. That's why none of Paul's Epistles emphasize the importance of works in relationship to a person's spiritual nature. Christian leaders who understand that it's Him, not them, stay consistent in Jesus. We've got to know where our dependency is.

We can't be like the Galatians. They started out with an understanding of the grace of God. They understood that they were made righteous by what He did, and not by their own works. But later, they thought that they had to add to His works in order to be more pleasing to God. This may sound strange to you, but—you're not ever going to be any more pleasing to God than you are right now! The more you awaken to who you are in Christ, the more you'll naturally do good works. It is natural for me to feel the love and the compassion that Jesus feels for people, because I'm one with Him. And the more I understand my oneness with Him, my acceptance by Him, the more I can love other people.

If you find yourself being increasingly critical towards others, I will guarantee that you are not receiving love from God for yourself. It's impossible to receive love and acceptance from God, then to turn around and be mean and critical to other people. I told you about the church that I used to belong to, the one that told me I was under the judgment of God. We left that church when we moved away to go to bible college, and on my very first day of class, I wept and wept. The teacher of the very first class session quoted the scripture, *"I did not come to judge and condemn the world, but that the world might have life."* I told God, "So you didn't come to judge me and condemn me—and I've been going through months and months of thinking I was under your judgment."

THE RIGHTEOUSNESS OF ABRAHAM

Abraham believed and trusted in God, and it was accredited to his account as righteousness. We know from the Word that he didn't have to keep the law in order to be considered righteous. It says he believed God. It's a good thing, too, because many of Abraham's actions got him in trouble. They certainly wouldn't have earned him a spot in heaven! But God looked at the things which be not as though they were. He looked at Abraham who had no righteousness in and of himself. Remember that Abraham was the one who lied on several occasions to save his own skin. Sojourning in a strange land, Abraham became fearful that men wanting his beautiful wife would kill him. So he lied to them, saying, "She's not my wife, she's my sister." Abraham was also the one who took the job of performing God's promise into his own hands. God promised him a son, an heir. But when his wife appeared unable to conceive, he had a child with her servant. This disobedience caused all kinds of problems!

But God looked at Abraham, who was fearful of man, and called him righteous. He looked at Abraham, who had inconsistency and disobedience in his life and said, "Abraham, you're righteous." God called the things that be not, as though they were, and not just in regard to Abraham's promised son. Sure, God looked at Abraham and said, "Okay, I know that you're an old man, unable to father a child. But I say that you're going to be a father of multitudes." But when God called the things that be not as though they were, He was referring to unrighteous Abraham, calling him righteous. And when Abraham believed that he had right standing with God—just because God said it, not because he earned it—his faith was accredited to him as righteousness.

By faith, we believe in Jesus. We believe in His sacrifice, we believe in what He did for us at the cross. We believe that God rose Jesus from the dead. We believe that Jesus became one with our sin. And in so doing, we not only have righteousness accounted to our account—we become the very righteousness of God in Christ.

Abraham believed when God spoke, telling him, "You're righteous." His strength was in believing the promises of God. I like the Scripture that says, "Abraham made the promises of God his own," (from Hebrews 11:17, and other scriptures). You and I must always make the promises of God our own and take the promises in the Word of God personally.

Hebrews 11:8-10 says, *"By faith Abraham, when he was called to go out into a place which he should after receive for an inheritance, obeyed; and he went out, not knowing whither he went."* Think about it—God tells Abraham that He wants him to go somewhere. And Abraham didn't even trouble his mind over it, because he trusted God. Hebrews 11 continues, *"By faith he sojourned in the land of promise, as in a strange country, dwelling in tabernacles with Isaac and Jacob, the heirs with him of the same promise: For he looked for a city which hath foundations, whose builder and maker is God."*

You're going to notice something that all great men and women of faith have in common. People who do great things for God are able to do so because they always keep their sights set on Him. They're able to tell themselves, "Hey, this situation is just temporary. My trust is in God and His Word." When problems occur, natural thinking tells us, "Here I go again. This is the way my life is. It's always going to be this way." But people of faith, like the "heroes of faith" mentioned in Hebrews, chapter 11, have discovered something powerful. They say, "We're temporary residents here. This is not our home. We're doing a service right now. We're doing what God has called us to do, and we can trust Him as we can keep our eyes on Him."

Consider Abraham, after he was told he had to sacrifice his son. He is drudging up the hill, so full of sorrow, probably thinking, "Oh, God, why are You making me do this?" But that's not the way it happened! Abraham trusted in God, for he had seen

God do the impossible. I believe that when God said, "I want you to sacrifice your son," anticipation born of faith rose up inside of him. Fear would have been the product of natural thinking, but faith produces something different. Faith says, "I'm trusting in God, and whatever He said to do, it's got to turn out good. I'll do whatever He said to do, because it's going to bring a blessing."

Hebrews 11:17 says, *"By faith Abraham, when he was tried, offered up Isaac: and he that had received the promises offered up his only begotten son."* Does this sound like somebody drudging up the hill to you? He *gladly* received the promises of God and was *ready* to sacrifice his son. The son of whom God said, "Through Isaac, your descendant, shall be reckoned." Abraham reasoned that God was able to raise Isaac up, even from among the dead. He didn't worry himself by saying, "I wonder what will happen?" Abraham encouraged himself, saying: "Wait a minute. God said my descendants would come from Isaac. Somehow, this has going to be fine." He reasoned in his mind, "God is able to raise a thousand Isaacs up."

He reasoned in his mind . . . So many times, when we hear something from God, we reason in our mind all the ways it couldn't work. We think of all the ways that it's going to be a "bummer." But Jesus said, from John 10:10, "I didn't come to take life away, but to give it—and to give it in abundance." Abraham *believed* God, and it was counted to him for righteousness. We can believe, too! We've been given right standing with God.

As believers, we've got to step out and believe in God because it's our nature to do so. According to the Word of God, we have the very faith *of* Jesus—the very faith of the Son of God. That enables us to step out on *anything*!

Romans 4:3 reminds us that Abraham believed and trusted in God and it was credited to his account as righteousness, right living and right standing with God. A laborer's wages are not considered a favor or as a gift, but rather as a debt, an obligation, something owed to him. But to one who is first, not under the Law, and second, trusts and believes fully in Him who justifies the ungodly, his faith is credited to him as righteousness, acceptable to God. David congratulates the man to whom God credits righteousness apart from the works that he does. He even pronounces a blessing over him: *"Blessed is he whose transgression is forgiven, whose sin is covered. Blessed is the man unto whom the Lord imputeth not iniquity."* —Psalms 32:1, 2a

Remember, "iniquity" means "guilt." Blessed—happy, fortunate, and to be envied—is the person whose sins the Lord will take no account of, nor reckon it against him. When writing this in Psalms, David foresaw that there would be a people who would have righteousness given to them without having to earn it. He says, "Congratulations to that guy. Congratulations to that people that would receive that."

Was this promise meant for only the circumcised, or was

it for the uncircumcised as well? We know that Abraham's faith was credited to him as righteousness. When did this occur? Was it before or after he had been circumcised? It was before, of course. That's important to know, because it shows us that Abraham didn't *do* anything to earn righteousness. It was given to him. It was not a wage. What God really said to Abraham is, "This is what I purpose, this is the decision that I'm making—you're righteous because you believed. You looked at My promises, you made them your own, and therefore I call you righteous."

As good as that was, there is still a difference between the righteousness that Abraham had and the righteousness that you and I have. For Abraham, righteousness was accredited to him. But you and I don't only have righteousness accredited to us and put to our account. We have it infused into us. Abraham couldn't become a new creation because Jesus hadn't died yet. All God could do is say, "It's as though he were like this." But you and I are not *as though* we were righteous. We *are* righteous. It's not *as though* we have the nature of God—we *do* have the nature of God. There's a difference between the way Abraham had righteousness and the way we have righteousness, because we're under a better covenant. We're under a better blessing because of Jesus!

Back to the book of Romans—in chapter 4, verse 13, it says, *"For the promise that he should be the heir to the world, was not to Abraham, or to his seed, through the law, but through the righteousness of faith."*

In the same way, you and I have the righteousness of faith. We have it simply because we believe what Jesus did. We believe that when He died, that He took upon everything that *I was* to become everything that *He is*. But righteousness has been imparted to us rather than just added to our account.

In Romans, Paul begins to make a distinction between the way things were (before being born again) and the way things are now (as new creations in Christ). Romans is a very important book when studying righteousness. In Chapter 5, verses 17, 18 and 19 demonstrate this: *"For if by one man's offense death reigned by one, much they which receive abundance of grace and of the gift of righteousness shall reign in life, by one, Jesus Christ. Therefore as by the offence of one judgment came upon all men to condemnation; even so by the righteousness of one the free gift came upon all men unto justification of life. For as by one man's disobedience many were made sinners, so by the obedience of one shall many be made righteous."*

The Law could only serve to expand and increase the trespass, making it more apparent. But when sin abounded, grace (God's unmerited favor) surpassed the sin. In the face of sin, grace increased all the more—grace super-abounded. Paraphrased, Paul says, "When Adam fell, when that offense that happened, death reigned." Think about all the people on this earth who have not received Jesus. Think about the way their lives are. It's as though death was still reigning, even though they have opportunity to receive Jesus right now—but it's worse when Christians walk as though death still reigned! But God said, "The offense brought death, but my abundance of grace will allow you to reign as kings!" Prophetically, Psalm 23 says, *"Yea, though I walk through the valley of the shadow of death, I fear no evil."*

Though I walk where other men, dead men, walk, I'm not fearful. Though I walk where people are not spiritually alive, I fear no evil. My God is with me!

THE RIGHTEOUSNESS OF PAUL

Paul's another one who knew how to take the Word of God personally. In Galatians 2:20, he referred to Jesus as, "The Son of God, who loved *me*, and gave Himself up for *me*."

Paul said things in the Word of God that most of would never think about saying. For instance, he said in Philippians 1:7, "Ye are all partakers of *my* grace." Just how many of us would be willing to say, "The world needs to receive *my* grace"? We wouldn't say something like that, but Paul took the things of God so personally, he thought of it as *his* grace. And in Romans 16:25, Paul says, "You are established by *my* gospel." Paul took the Gospel personally!

Notice how Paul talked about himself. He'd say, "I'm like a father to you," (from 1 Thessalonian 2:11). Who else describes himself that way? God does! And Paul says, *"I must again suffer the birth pains for you as my dear beloved children who I have begotten,"* (Galatians 4:19). Paul talked like Jesus talked. He did so because he understood that when he became a Christian, he became one with God. He believed everything that belonged to God was his, too. He took his role as minister of reconciliation very seriously.

The very nature of God—the essence of who God is—transformed the nature of who Paul was. That's why Paul was able to truthfully say, *"I am crucified with Christ: nevertheless I live; yet not I, but Christ liveth in me: and the life which I now live in the flesh I live by the faith of the Son of God, who loved me, and gave himself for me,"* (Galatians 2:20).

"It's no longer I who live, but Christ." You and I need to get to the point where we can say the same thing as assertively as Paul can. We need to make some bold proclamations about ourselves. We need to say the same things about ourselves that the Word of God says about us.

THE FIGHT OF FAITH

As we begin to let our faith rise up concerning this subject of righteousness, I want to tell you something. This is one of the most important studies that we will ever do. Did you know that the "fight of faith" the Bible talks about is not the fight *for* faith. You've heard it said, "You know, old so-and-so doesn't have enough faith." But that can't be true—at least, according to the word of God it can't! It's not that a person doesn't have enough faith. If they believe in Jesus, they have enough faith. They just may not know how to activate the faith of Jesus that is resident in them.

My Bible says that I live by the faith *of* the Son of God who loved me and gave Himself up for me. The fight that we have is the same fight that Jesus had, the same fight He had with the devil, and it was about His identity—who He *really* was.

The devil came to Him and said, "*If* you are the Son of God . . ." Of course, the devil knew that He was the Son of God. He was trying to put doubt in His mind. Later, when Jesus stood before Pilate, he said, "They *say* you're a king. Who do you say that you are?" Now, if Jesus looked at His circumstances right at that moment, He would have to say, "I'm nothing. I'm a failure." But Jesus, holding up that shield of faith, said, "I am as you say that I am."

It's very important that, as we look in the word of God, we see our identity. We must realize that the fight that we're going to have is a fight about who we are in Christ—about our righteousness, about our right standing with God. Unfortunately, it's the church and our brethren in Christ who fight the hardest to convince us otherwise. That's a trap that many Christians and many churches fall into. They imagine that their "ministry" is to show everything that people are doing wrong, and that they need to get it right before God. But remember—and we've discussed this—righteous works never produce righteousness. But righteousness, which is our state of being, will produce righteous works!

Jesus taught about the fight *of* faith, but for some reason, we began to think He was talking about a fight *for* faith. We incorrectly tell ourselves, "I have got to have more faith. I just don't have enough." The Bible tells us that we have *the very faith of the Son of God who loved us and gave Himself up for us* (Galatians 2:20). If we have the faith of Jesus, how is it that we need more faith? We don't! We have all the faith that we need. We have the very faith of Jesus Himself.

The fight of faith says that you and I never need to back down from what the Word of God says—no matter what we're feeling, no matter what somebody else says about us. The fight of faith says, *"Let God* (and His Word) *be true, but every man a liar,"* (Romans 3:4). There are times when people will try to absolutely crush your hopes and dreams. But you've got a God living in you that'll make those hopes and dreams spring back up, stronger than ever before.

There's a story that I heard John Osteen tell a number of years ago. He said that if a bird's wing should break, it's a terrible thing. But when that bird heals, the wing is so strong in the place it broke that it can never be broken in that place again. Like the bird's wing, perhaps there are areas where you've been hurt and broken; never to fly again. But if we'll just fight the fight of faith; if we allow God to heal us, those impaired, damaged and broken areas will be made stronger than they were before; so strong can never be broken there again!

THE TREE OF LIFE

Jesus didn't come to judge and condemn. Here's how God judges: *"I judge you made whole. I judge you set free from sin. I judge you righteous."* Proverbs 11:30 says, *"The fruit of the righteous is a tree of life; and he that winneth souls is wise."* It says the "fruit of the righteous." Now, who are the righteous? We are! We're righteous.

Other Scriptures which speak of "a tree of life" include Proverbs 15:4, which says *"a wholesome tongue is a tree of life."* But let's look at the first reference about the "tree of life," found in Genesis 2:9, *"And out of the ground made the LORD God to grow every tree that is pleasant to the sight, and good for food; the tree of life also in the midst of the garden, and the tree of knowledge of good and evil."*

The tree of life was given to Adam and Eve to freely partake from. But it was not permissible for them to eat of the tree of the knowledge of good and evil. Genesis 2:16 says, *"And the*

LORD God commanded the man, saying, Of every tree of the garden thou mayest freely eat: But of the tree of the knowledge of good and evil, thou shalt not eat of it: for in the day that thou eatest thereof thou shalt surely die." You know the rest of the story—Adam and Eve were successfully tempted to eat of that forbidden tree. When they did so, they immediately experienced spiritual death. Furthermore, their bodies began to die the moment they disobeyed God. They became one with sin.

Mercifully, God drove them out of the garden so they could no longer eat of the tree of life. Had they continued to eat of the tree of life in their fallen state, man would have remained in that state of damnation forever. Their bodies would begin to show forth the results of their sin nature, and all manners of disease and sickness would manifest. Yet they would still be alive in their bodies. It would be better for Adam and Eve to die, thereby escaping this horror.

The word "tree" in the Greek, the language of the New Testament, does not mean trees in the way we might imagine. "Tree" (stauros) means a cross or a pole. Acts 5:30 says, *"The God of our fathers raised up Jesus, whom ye slew and hanged on a tree."* The tree is the cross. Acts 10:39 says, *"And we are witnesses of all things which he did both in the land of the Jews, and in Jerusalem; whom they slew and hanged on a tree."*

The following Scriptures powerfully reveal our position in

Christ. Gal 3:13 says, *"Christ hath redeemed us from the curse of the law, being made a curse for us: for it is written, Cursed is every one that hangeth on a tree."* He became my punishment, a curse for me. That's why He hung on a tree—He took my place. And 1 Peter 2:24 says, *"Who his own self bare our sins in his own body on the tree; that we, being dead to sins, should live unto righteousness: by whose stripes ye were healed."*

Do you see the powerful symbolism here? In the garden, the fruit of a tree caused the fall of man. But redemption came through the "fruit of a tree" when Jesus gave His life for mankind on the cross. The tree of life in the garden was taken from mankind because of the fall. But another tree, the cross that crucified Christ, became our tree of life. Isn't God's plan for redemption incredible? The eternal sacrifice that Jesus made on the cross gives us the very *Zoe* life of God.

Through the greatest tragedy of all of history—the fall of man—God has blessed us! What we experience as New Testament believers is so much more than just the return of what Adam lost. Revelation 2:7 says it best, *"He that hath an ear, let him hear what the Spirit saith unto the churches; To him that overcometh will I give to eat of the tree of life, which is in the midst of the paradise of God."* God has made us to overcome, because we can partake of the tree of life, which is the cross of Christ. The tree of life in heaven is the cross of Jesus. Revelation 22:2 says, *"In the midst of the street of it, and on either side of the river, was there the tree of life, which bare twelve manner of fruits, and yielded her fruit every month:*

and the leaves of the tree were for the healing of the nations." The cross of Jesus gives us life, God's kind and quality of life. This life includes the provision for healing in every area of our being. Thanks be to Jesus, we don't have to wait to get to heaven to partake of the tree of life. We can partake of the cross—the tree of life—all the time. ❧

PART III

•••

Reconciliation

"God has given us the task of telling everyone what He is doing. We're Christ's representatives. God uses us to persuade men and women to drop their differences and enter into God's work of making things right between them. We're speaking for Christ Himself now: Become friends with God; He's already a friend with you."

— 2 Corinthians 5:18 —
The Message Bible

THE MINISTRY OF RECONCILIATION

Righteousness speaks. Righteousness has a voice. As we began to listen, we discover what righteousness *is* saying and this is what *it's not* saying. It's not saying, "Jesus, please come down from Heaven and heal us. Jesus, please come up from the bottom of the earth and help us." Righteousness says, "It's all been done. The word of faith is right here on my lips and in my mouth. I can call forth things that be not as though they were."

Sometimes, in our thinking, we completely separate the persons of God the Father, God the Son, and God the Holy Spirit. Of course, the Bible tells us that they are the Godhead, Three in One. You'll hear people say that the word "trinity" is not found in the Bible. That's correct! But we do find the word "godhead," meaning God the Father, God the Son, and God the Holy Spirit as One. And as we think about those three separate persons, it's easy to look at Jesus as the "good guy," always trying to appease God the Father in our behalf. After all, it was Jesus Who made the supreme sacrifice at the cross! But remember, it pleased God the Father to send Jesus so that He could take our place and be the sacrifice.

As we begin to see things as God sees them, we will find that we don't look at other people from a merely human viewpoint, or from a natural point of view. I can't even look at myself that way, saying, "After all, I'm only human—that's why things happen to me." According to God, you're spirit. The fullness of the Godhead dwells in you and me.

People used to look at Jesus and say, "Hey, there's Joseph's son, the carpenter. That's Mary's son." And because they looked at Him from a natural point of view, they missed out on the blessings of God. Remember when Jesus went to his hometown, and everybody said, "Isn't this Mary's son?" Consequently, He could only do a few miracles there. People did not recognize that He was the Christ.

When the Bible mentions "Jesus Christ," the word "Christ" refers to the anointing of God. Christ is the anointed of God, come in the form of man. When you see the word "Jesus," the Bible is usually speaking about the physical man Jesus. Scripture says that we once regarded Jesus from a human viewpoint, but now, we should regard Him—and no other person, for that matter—from a human point of view. If you and I would stop seeing ourselves from a human viewpoint and see ourselves from God's point-of-view, we would move in great power. God has always meant for mankind to move in His great power, at all times and in every situation.

"Therefore if any man be in Christ, he is a new creature: old things are passed away; behold, all things are become new." Consider for a moment your old way of thinking, of living, of being. What you used to be has passed away. Actually, we shouldn't even consider that which used to be. The Bible says we should forget it! It's correct in religious circles to say, "I'm just a sinner saved by grace." But the truth is, old things have passed away. Our concentration needs to be on "the fresh and new that is come" (from 2 Corinthians 5:17).

God is looking for us to get our minds renewed to what He's already done. His nature is to give, not to take away. In Acts, whenever a group of people went out to minister, they would go forth to heal the sick and give something to the people they were ministering to. Jesus said, "I didn't come to take life away but to give it," (from John 10:10). If we think God is primarily interested in dealing with *our* sinful actions, we'll be primarily interested in making others stop *their* sin actions. We'll try to get them to stop doing wrong so they, too, can be pleasing to God. But that's the wrong message—that's not the Gospel. We're supposed to be telling them about the goodness of God and walking in our ministry of reconciliation.

We treat ourselves the same way—somehow, we think that we're our own keepers, that we belong to us, that we're responsible to work out our own salvation by ourselves. We're ready to be the good soldier, ready to get ourselves in line. But I found out something—I can't make me get in line. Not all the time, not in every situation. If I were able to get myself in line, I wouldn't have needed Jesus! All I can do is submit myself to Him. He's the One who has made my path straight.

All things are from God, who, through Jesus Christ, has reconciled us to Himself. He's received us into His favor and brought us into harmony with Himself. In turn, He's given us the "ministry of condemnation," that by word or deed we might aim to bring others into harmony with Him. Right? Oops—I guess I must be reading from the "Exaggerated Translation" of the Bible. Hopefully, your Bible reads a little different. The ministry God has given us is the *ministry of reconciliation*. We have a ministry which tells people they can be one with God the Father because of what Jesus has done. By word and deed, we show that we can live in harmony with Him and with others.

It was God, personally present in Christ, Who reconciled and restored the world to favor with Him. Not counting up or holding against men their trespasses, but canceling them. That message of reconciliation, of restoration and favor, has been committed to us, the Body of Christ. We're to preach it to the world—we're Christ's ambassadors, His personal representatives. God makes His appeal to mankind through us. For His sake, we tell the world to lay hold of the divine favor now offered by God, and to be reconciled to Him. We preach that He made Christ, who knew no sin, to be sin. And, through Him, we might be endued with—and viewed as examples of—the righteousness of God. We, then, ought to live life in right relationship with Him and with His approval and favor.

Ministry that condemns people for the wrong things they do, and that tells people that God is mad at them because of their actions, is not conveying the message that we're supposed to be sharing. God doesn't hate people who have abortions. God doesn't hate homosexuals. Now, because of Jesus and the cross, nobody has to be in bondage to these sins—or to any other sin, for that matter. But God doesn't hate sinners. The Gospel message is a message of reconciliation. Anyone can be reconciled to God, and anything can be made right. Jesus did it all! Now the only thing left to do is to receive.

THE SACRIFICE

Jesus, who knew no sin, became sin, so that we could become the righteousness of God (says 2 Corinthians 5:21). Jesus did not *do* sin. He didn't perform sin. He didn't practice sin—he *became* sin. In the same way, you and I don't *do* actions of righteousness to become righteous. It's an exchange. He became sin; we become righteous.

But when you think about Jesus and His sacrifice, remember—He was God, personally present in Christ, who reconciled the world to Himself. Remember that this act of redemption involves more than Jesus being the "good guy" setting out to appease the God the Father in our behalf. God the Father, God the Son, and God the Holy Spirit all have the same thing in mind—to unify us with Him, and with one another, as family. God had an extreme desire to see us become righteous, to have a nature that is right with Him—the same nature as Jesus, so we can access the Father. That desire was so great that Jesus suffered death at the cross.

What an injustice it would be, for you and I to know of God's great desire to see mankind redeemed, to know the depth of the physical suffering Jesus experienced, to know of the greatness of the eternal life secured for us by that sacrifice—and then, for us to render all of this as insignificant by believing that righteousness and the new birth could be secured by our own good works or righteous acts! It is clear that God had to show love and compassion, and dedication and sacrifice, when He redeemed mankind from sin's deadly grasp. What futility there is in thinking that our performance somehow contributes to God's plan in the redemption.

According to the Word of God, there's only one noteworthy "right action"—to receive Jesus as Savior and Lord by faith. So, then, it must be true that one does not go back into the kingdom of darkness by committing sin. We've been birthed into the kingdom of light. Wrong actions do not change our state of being. And as we begin to understand our righteous state of being, we'll stop having trouble with wrong actions. Really! We concentrate so much on the *actions;* God concentrates on one's *state of being.* My state of being will cause me to act accordingly. But when we don't understand that we've become righteous, we'll always be trying to accomplish something God has already done.

God cares about us so much. He wants us to walk in freedom. I Timothy 3 tells us, "Don't get entangled again in the yoke of bondage that you used to be in." Jesus has set us free. And, the Bible says that if the Son has set you free, you're free indeed! You're free in reality. The 16th verse of 1 Timothy, chapter 3 says, *"And without controversy great is the mystery of godliness: God was manifest in the flesh, justified in the Spirit, seen of angels, preached unto the Gentiles, believed on in the world, received up into glory."*

Who does it say did this? God did. All the different translations
I'm aware of read, "He, God" or "God did this".

JESUS MADE TO "BE" SIN

Here's a question for you. How did Adam go from righteousness to unrighteousness? It was through sin. Many gen-
erations later, Jesus became sin. At that time, Jesus went from
righteousness to unrighteousness. How? No one could have
killed Jesus. No one could have taken His life. Not that they
didn't try! Do you remember when Jesus preached in the syn-
agogue, proclaiming that Isaiah chapter 61 had been fulfilled in
their hearing? An angry mob took Him outside of the town to
kill Him. But He escaped by walking right through them! How
was that possible? There was a supernatural anointing on Him,
and He could not be killed before His time. In fact, when Pilate
said, "I have the authority to take your life," in John 19, verses 10
and 11, Jesus said, "You don't have the authority to take it, but I
can give it."

The Word of God says that God came in the flesh and was
vindicated or justified in the spirit (1 Timothy 3:16). Now, if He
had to be vindicated or justified in spirit, then He must have literally been made to be sin at some point (just like the Bible says).
You know, there's a big controversy in Christianity over this issue—but I really don't understand why. Some Christian theolo-

gians maintain that He became sin without giving up His righteous nature. Now if that were true, why would Jesus, who came in the flesh, have to be justified in the spirit? He would have to be justified in the spirit only if He had been made unrighteous—in the spirit. God would never have to be brought *back* to a state of righteousness unless it was something He had genuinely given up in our behalf.

When Jesus came to this earth, He was just as righteous as He was in Heaven. Wouldn't you agree? But something happened. When Jesus gave up His life at Calvary, He became one with sin. He became subject to the consequence of sin, which first and foremost is death. He became one with Satan, in the same way that we were one with Satan when we entered into this world. That's why you see darkness fall upon the whole earth on Good Friday afternoon. There are those that will say, "He couldn't have been made sin. Our God would never do that." But there's nothing that God would require of you and me that He has not already required of Himself. More importantly, there is nothing we could do to redeem ourselves from sin and its penalty. Whatever Jesus *did do* for us at Calvary, we could benefit from. But whatever He *didn't do* for us, we would have to do for ourselves. And if that were the case, we'd still be unredeemed!

It would be impractical, impossible, and down-right unjust for God to say, "Claudia, transform yourself from your unrighteous state." I was born into unrighteousness. Jesus knew that

He'd have to do it for me. Once again, be reminded that I'm talking about *God*. *God* came down in the flesh. God, whose righteousness and holiness distinguish Him from any other being in all of creation, laid it down for me. Such is the extent of His love for us! From His desire for us to be seated next to Him, to be joint heirs with Him, and to be right with Him, He laid down His life—His very nature of life—for us.

I'm making this point to convince you of God's great goodness. Not that you'd disagree, of course—but I'm sure you've heard people preach otherwise. Why is it that some folks will fight tooth and nail to prove how *bad* God is? Why will some argue with all the vigor they can muster to try to convince others that God is a *mean* God? Perhaps it's because, somehow, the Gospel sounds too good to be true . . .

When Abraham heard the promise of God, he laughed the laugh of faith. But Sarah, upon hearing the same promise, laughed the laugh of unbelief. She didn't think it was possible that God could be that caring, or maybe she just didn't think that He was able to make good on His promise. Either way, some people find that it's easier to reject a free gift from God than to simply receive it from Him. Not me—I know that receiving a gift is easier that earning it.

"For Christ also hath once suffered for sins, the just for the unjust, that he might bring us to God, being put to death in the flesh, but

quickened by the Spirit:" (I Peter 3:18). In His human body, He was put to death. But He was made alive again in spirit. But—why would Jesus have to be made alive in spirit? Because He was dead in spirit. That's how He became our sacrifice. He allowed Himself to become sin. You know already that life and death cannot exist in the same human body. Like the Bible says—a person can't be salty and fresh at the same time, or light and dark at the same time. Righteousness and unrighteousness cannot exist at the same time in the same person. Jesus became one with darkness so you and I could become one with light. If that wasn't true, why does the Bible say that He was made alive in the spirit?

We also know that Jesus, when He became one with our sin, went into hell. The Bible tells us that He threw off all principalities and powers and that He stripped Satan of all authority and power (read Colossians 2:15). Once again, many Christian theologians would say, "Well, I just don't believe Jesus went to hell." But if Jesus didn't go to hell and pay our penalty, then we still have to!

Let's look in the Word of God and see what He says about the matter. Going back again to 1 Peter 3:19, the Bible says, *"By which also he went and preached unto the spirits in prison; Which sometime were disobedient, when once the longsuffering of God waited in the days of Noah, while the ark was a preparing, wherein few, that is, eight souls were saved by water."*

Do you believe what the Bible says? Certainly—and here's the Bible, talking about Jesus going down and preaching to the captives. Remember—if Jesus didn't go to hell, pay our ransom, and become our victor—we still have to do it! But I have news for you. Jesus already has done it. When Jesus died on the cross, I died on that cross. You died on that cross. When Jesus stripped Satan of all power and authority, I stripped Satan of all power and authority. I'm in Christ. It's just as if I did it myself.

Still not convinced? Let's look at some more Scriptures. You say, "I don't want to get into these doctrinal things." Oh, yes, but sometimes these "doctrinal things" are important. The word "doctrine" is not a bad word. Paul says, "I want you to believe the doctrines that I have laid before you." The doctrines of man—now, that's a different matter. Doctrines of man are a bad thing, so let's look at Bible doctrine instead.

In Acts 2:27, we find a prophetic Word that David was speaking about Jesus, saying, *Because thou wilt not leave my soul in hell, neither wilt thou suffer thine Holy One to see corruption.* And, in verse 31, *He seeing this before spake of the resurrection of Christ, that his soul was not left in hell, neither his flesh did see corruption.*

Isn't it interesting that this prophecy was brought forth in the New Testament, while talking about the death of Jesus? As David gave this prophecy, he was saying, "You'll not allow Jesus to stay in hell. You'll be able to bring Him up from there."

Yes, Jesus went into hell—but then He received the spirit of righteousness. The Book of Nicodemus (not a book of the Bible, but an interesting account, nevertheless) says that when Jesus received that spirit of righteousness, He stood up—and, as He did so, it says that demons screamed and angels shouted. Then He burst through the wall with laughter and began to take total authority over Satan. What a perfect depiction of Jesus' time in hell! Satan is depicted as being so full of fear! Satan and Beelzebub begin to argue and bicker with each other because they're very scared. They see that not only is Jesus taking power and authority over them, but everybody that believes upon Jesus begins to do the same! Whether this book was really written by Nicodemus as the result of a vision or not, I don't know. But I do know this—I do know that Jesus has power and authority over the devil.

POWER & AUTHORITY OVER THE DEVIL

Now, before Jesus ever came to this earth, He already had power and authority over the devil. So why did He have to go through all of this? It's because you and I did not have power and authority over the devil. Jesus became one with us, one with mankind. He won victory over death and hell so that *His* victory would be *our* victory.

According to the Word of God, He preached while He was

in hell. The Word says His soul was not left in hell, nor did his flesh see corruption. Once again, if we don't see and understand this truth, we're going to think that there still is a price to be paid. Jesus paid that price once and for all!

Jesus had been in authority over Satan for all eternity, but He came to earth as a man so that you and I could also have power and authority over Satan. When the disciples got a glimpse of the day when man would have authority over Satan in Luke 10: 19, Jesus said, *"Behold, I give unto you power to tread on serpents and scorpions, and over all the power of the enemy: and nothing shall by any means hurt you."*

There was a time where all men feared demonic oppression because the devil and his horde did pretty well as they pleased on this earth. But thank God for the message of reconciliation, which says, "God has taken of Satan, and he has no power over me and no authority over me. Nothing in me belongs to Satan." The message that the Holy Spirit speaks to the world is, "Satan has been judged. Jesus has obtained righteousness for us. Mankind now needs to believe upon Jesus Christ as Lord and Savior."

When Jesus arose from the dead, He arose in complete and total victory. He conquered death. He defeated sin. He rendered sickness, poverty, oppression, and every other enemy of man powerless. He rose up in perfect righteousness. No sin; no sickness, pain or disease followed Him out of the grave. Think about it—Jesus didn't rise from the dead in the same physical state as He was before going to the cross! He came back in a body glorified. But, it was a man's body, nevertheless.

When Stephen was being stoned, he looked up and he said, *"Behold! I see the heavens opened, and the Son of man standing on the right hand of God,"* (Acts 7:56). He said, "the Son of man." Do you know that forever and always, there is a man in Heaven named Christ Jesus? Before Jesus came to this earth, there was not a man in Heaven. There was Christ the Son of God in Heaven, but not a man. But now in heaven, there is a man Christ Jesus. He became just like us—spirit and flesh. A man! Romans 6:4-5 says, *"Therefore we are buried with him by baptism into death: that like as Christ was raised up from the dead by the glory of the Father, even so we also should walk in newness of life. For if we have been planted together in the likeness of his death, we shall be also in the likeness of his resurrection."*

When He rose again, He rose again into total righteousness, into a state of being that was absolutely right with God. When He received the spirit of righteousness, that spirit determined who He was. He was in total authority over any power of the enemy, total victory over sickness. You ask, "But didn't He already have total authority over everything?" Yes, from the beginning of time, the Son of God had all heavenly authority. But now it was different. Now the man, Jesus Christ, had it. What's more, we can have it, because we have become absolutely one with Him.

In the mind of God, when He died, we died. Satan is afraid of the believer because in the realm of the spirit, Satan doesn't know the difference between Christ and us. We're absolutely one. Because we've been planted together in the likeness of His death, we shall also be in the likeness of His resurrection. We've been recreated into His likeness, which has brought us a righteous standing that is absolutely equal to that of Christ Jesus Himself.

He died in sin, but He arose in victory. He raised in freedom, He raised in power, He raised in might, He raised in every glorious thing that God has. And as He did, you and I did the same. The first chapter of the Book of Revelation speaks of His mighty victory. Perhaps we've overlooked just how powerful a victory it is! In it, Jesus gives a description of Himself today. He says, "I am the Ever-living One. I am living in the eternity of the eternities. I died, but see—I am alive forevermore. I possess the keys of death and Hades, or hell, the realm of the dead."

I kept thinking about this. He's saying, "Look—I am He who was dead, but here I am in the eternity of eternities. I'm alive forevermore. But I want to tell you what else happened. I now possess the keys of death and hell!" And as I thought about it, I remembered something else Jesus said. He tells His disciples, *"I give you the keys of the kingdom. Whatsoever things you bind on earth are already bound in Heaven; whatsoever things you loose on earth are already loosed in Heaven."* —Matthew 16:18

Jesus has given us keys of death and hell. This death does not refer to physical death—He's talking about spiritual death. You and I have the keys this world needs so it can get out of the bondage of spiritual death. Righteousness speaks, remember? Righteousness says, "It's a done deal. You don't have to be spiritually dead. You can be spiritually alive because of what Jesus has done. He's alive forevermore, but *you* can be alive forevermore." This is the message we're supposed to take to the world. When He says, "I've given you the keys of death," we can identify that spiritual death in people's lives, then loose the very life of God. We can do that by the preaching of the Gospel.

The keys that Jesus gave us were not physical keys. They were spiritual keys, and those spiritual keys are activated by the "word of faith that is nigh thee, even in our mouths." Those keys work as we speak to situations. Our words let the power of God loose! He also said, "I've given you the keys of death," and, "I've given you the keys of hell." God never intended for any man to go to hell. Hell was fabricated for the devil and his angels. The saddest Scripture that I know of in the whole Bible is the one that says, "Hell had to be enlarged to contain all the souls that were going there." But you and I have a key that's been given to us. We can lock up hell so that mankind need never go there. We do it through the preaching of the Gospel.

The Bible tells us that we're preachers. All of us! When Paul says in 2 Timothy 4:2 to *"Herald and preach the word,"* he's not talking about standing behind the pulpit. That word "herald" is an army term. If two armies were fighting a battle, a herald would go from one side of the battlefield to the other with a message of peace, saying, "We don't want to have this war any longer." You and I are the heralds of heaven. We have come to the world with a message of peace—God is not angry. God is not mad. His wrath has already been poured out on sin through Jesus Christ at the cross, and what's being offered to the world is peace, joy and righteousness in the Holy Spirit. That's the ministry of reconciliation. Wherever we go, we go with the message of peace, the message of what Jesus has already done for us.

Understand that Jesus doesn't have need of those keys in heaven. We have need of the keys right here on earth, and He's given them to us. And righteousness continues to speak. *"And what is the exceeding greatness of his power to us-ward who believe, according to the working of his mighty power, Which he wrought in Christ, when he raised him from the dead, and set him at his own right hand in the heavenly places, Far above all principality, and power, and might, and dominion, and every name that is named, not only in this world, but also in that which is to come."* —Ephesians 1:19-21

It goes on to say, "He has put all things under His feet." And, by virtue of us being in Christ, when Christ died for sin and was resurrected, it says God gave *us* that position and authority. God's plan ensured that all principalities and powers would be far below where He was. But, by virtue of us being in Christ, we are now seated in heavenly places with Him. By virtue of us being in Christ, principalities and powers are far below us, and they have no power or authority over us. Just like with Jesus, they're below us. Far below!

The Bible tells us that, even when we were dead in sin, He quickened us together with Christ, raised us up together, and made us sit in Heavenly places in and with Christ Jesus. We need to understand that the very life of Jesus is living in us right now. The resurrected life, full of victory, full of power—the life that has overcome all obstacles is inside you and me. Jesus said it this way, "Out of your belly shall flow rivers of living water." He was talking about the rivers of "Zoe"—the rivers of the very life of God Himself. He's saying, "Within you is the very life, the victorious life of God." You and I have no reason to ever walk in defeat, or to ever walk oppressed of the devil.

Before we discuss some of the prophecies about what Jesus would do in regard to our righteousness, I want to remind you what the definition of "righteousness" is. First, what it's not—it is *not* an action. It is a state of being, of being made right and clean before God. About righteous works—Righteousness is my state of being, me being made right before God, and it will allow me to have the power to do right works. But, remember—right works will never produce a righteous state of being in me. The Bible says we were born again unto righteousness. That happened at the new birth. We became new creations, having been made right before God. E. W. Kenyon describes it as "the ability to stand before God without a sense of guilt or inferiority." You and I don't need to ever harbor feelings of guilt or inferiority. We don't ever need to be conscious of sin.

Do you remember the trap I told you about? I warned you about listening to people who are always talking about the sins that other people do. I don't need to know about all the sins that people do. I don't need to hear about the sins that *I* do, either! You see, I'm real good at sin. I am, and I already know it! What I need to hear about is the change of nature that has happened inside of me. I haven't had nearly enough practice in knowing how to act out of my righteous nature.

The thing that Satan loves to do is to have Christians concentrate on all the wrong things. He wants Christians to concentrate on all the things that still need to be corrected in them. But God is saying, "I want you to behold the fresh and the new that is come. I want your concentration to be on the fact that you've been made right. You've been perfected. You are a holy people. At one time, you were not a people, but now you are a people. I want you to know that there is no condemnation for those who walk after the Spirit."

God wants us to move into the place where we don't have any sense of sin in our lives. You could sit down with just about any group of Christians and say, "Write down all of the things that God needs to change in your life"—and they could easily write a long list of their shortcomings. But the truth of the matter is, He's already changed them, and old things have passed away. We are to behold the fresh and the new that is come. This is what freedom is—if you're asked, "What things does God need to change in you?" And you should reply, "Nothing—I'm going from one degree of glory to another degree of glory, to another degree of glory!"

Abraham had righteousness given to him. It was accredited to him, and not because he did righteous works, but because Abraham believed. Even so, we have a righteousness that's better than Abraham's. Righteousness is not only accredited to my account; it's been imputed to me. It's *become* me. It's become my nature.

It's like saying, on the one hand, "There's a bill that you owe, but you don't have to pay it." But it would be better if someone came and told us, "Here—I give you the money to pay the bill, and a whole lot more." Righteousness has become who I am. And if we understand who we are, we'll never think, "Oh, God, I've been forsaken of you." We'll never think, "I'm not enough, I'm not good enough," or, "God's mad at me, I just know He is." Righteousness produces the anticipation of good things coming from God. Righteousness always has a sense of well being—it is the confidence that everything is right in our relationship with God.

MORE ABOUT THE SACRIFICE

Psalm 22 gives us a picture of Jesus during His time on the cross. It's a prophecy that was chronicled before Jesus went to the cross, written many years before Jesus ever came to the earth. And even though many of the people who followed Jesus had read and studied those words, revelation hadn't been given to them that Jesus was the fulfillment of this and other Messianic prophecies. Who would have ever thought God that would be *so* good? That He would not require us to do all the right things to be with Him? That He would give Himself to be the Sacrifice for mankind? The difference between Christianity and any other religion is that other religions require a sacrifice from the people. But in reality, God sacrificed Himself. This makes God, and Christianity, unique.

Psalm 22 shows us what it was like for Jesus to be separated from the Father. He became one with our sin. Not the *action* of sin, but with the *state of being* of sin. When we were born in this world, we were born into sin. We weren't born into doing the action of sin. Sin was our nature—we were born into sin. Jesus said it this way, "Your father is the devil." And our father, the devil, birthed us into sin. Now, Jesus became that very nature of sin. He became as though Satan was His very father and master. In Psalm 22, He cries out:

My God, my God, why hast thou forsaken me? Why art thou so far from helping me, and from the words of my roaring?

O my God, I cry in the day time, but thou hearest not; and in the night season, and am not silent.

But thou art holy, O thou that inhabitest the praises of Israel.

Our fathers trusted in thee: they trusted, and thou didst deliver them.

They cried unto thee, and were delivered: they trusted in thee, and were not confounded.

But I am a worm, and no man; a reproach of men, and despised of the people.

All they that see me laugh me to scorn: they shoot out the lip, they shake the head, saying,

He trusted on the LORD that he would deliver him: let him deliver him, seeing he delighted in him.

But thou art he that took me out of the womb: thou didst make me hope when I was upon my mother's breasts.

I was cast upon thee from the womb: thou art my God from my mother's belly.

Be not far from me; for trouble is near; for there is none to help.

Many bulls have compassed me: strong bulls of Bashan have

beset me round.

They gaped upon me with their mouths, as a ravening and a roaring lion.

I am poured out like water, and all my bones are out of joint: my heart is like wax; it is melted in the midst of my bowels.

My strength is dried up like a potsherd; and my tongue cleaveth to my jaws; and thou hast brought me into the dust of death.

For dogs have compassed me: the assembly of the wicked have enclosed me: they pierced my hands and my feet.

I may tell all my bones: they look and stare upon me.

They part my garments among them, and cast lots upon my vesture.

But be not thou far from me, O LORD: O my strength, haste thee to help me.

This was Jesus' cry when He was on the cross. For the first time in all of eternity, Jesus experienced what sin was. We know that for eternity, Jesus had always been holy. He had been just like God the Father. He was righteous and pure, and He had experienced nothing but unbroken fellowship with God the Father. Even on the earth, we saw Jesus walk in joy and peace. He had a perfect sense of righteousness. Regardless of circumstances, He understood that there was nothing that He could ask the

Father that the Father would deny Him. Jesus understood His righteousness allowed Him to go before God at any time and say, *"God, I know You hear me and You always hear me."* There was never a time when Jesus felt condemnation, or insecure, or forsaken of God, or where Jesus felt like God didn't hear Him.

But when on the cross, Jesus begins to say, *"My God, My God, why have you forsaken me?"* Through Him, we begin to see what unrighteousness is like. The Bible says the Lord is far from the wicked. But when Jesus became one with wickedness, one with sin, and one with our nature, He became far from God. Jesus said, "I feel forsaken of You."

In Psalm 22:6, He says, *"I am a worm, and no man."* The term "no man" refers to one who is shamed and mocked by others. The Bible says in Proverbs 13:5, *"A wicked man is loathsome and comes to shame."* Jesus says, "Lord, I trusted You. I want to be delivered!" But the Word of God says, *"The expectation of the wicked shall perish,"* in Proverbs 10:28. On the cross, Jesus felt just like the wicked do—forsaken of God. All hope is gone, and He was the mockery of all people.

The word "worm" as used in Psalm 22 deserves our attention. It refers to a female worm, scarlet or crimson in color. Now when the female of the scarlet worm species is ready to give birth to her young, she attaches her body to the trunk of a tree. She fixes herself so firmly and permanently to that tree, she can never

leave again. The egg is deposited beneath her body, which pro-
tects it until the larva is hatched and able to enter into their own
life circle. When the mother worm dies, a crimson fluid from her
body stains the surrounding wood. Commercial scarlet dyes are
extracted from the dead bodies of these worms.

What a clear picture this gives us of Christ on the cross!
He gave his life on the tree, shedding precious blood so that He
might bring many sons into glory. He died for us so we might
live through Him. Just as the female "worm" that attached herself to the wood of the tree and gave her life so that she could give
life to others, Jesus attached Himself to the tree and gave His life
so that He could give us new birth. Isn't it interesting that this
worm was a commercial source of the color scarlet? And that it
would leave a permanent mark on the tree?

The blood of Jesus is why you and I are free. When we
look at the plan of God, we see that Jesus was forsaken of God
so that we would never have to be forsaken by Him. Because Jesus said, *"You're far from me,"* you and I would never have to be
far from God. If we would get hold of a real sense of righteousness—if we would grasp the reality of who we are in Christ—
there will never be a time when you and I feel separated from
God or forsaken of Him.

There will also never be a time when the wrath of God will
be poured out upon us. That's something that just could never

happen. In the prophecies describing the sacrifice of Jesus, we're told that He took God's wrath for us. That way, we could stand before God and say, "My God, my God, you've heard me. Now I am somebody. I was not a people, and You have made me a people." That's why we need never feel like we're forsaken of God. Stop receiving things that we've been delivered from!

If we don't acknowledge the grace of God in our lives—if we refuse to give it the consideration it is due by trying in some way to redeem ourselves through our own goodness—it's as if the grace of God doesn't exist. We make it powerless and render it as ineffective. I don't ever want to make a blessing from God ineffective or inactive in my life. I need His blessings—all of them! Besides, Jesus paid a price—a high price—so we'd be able to walk in fullness of life.

This was God's plan from the very first day God ever thought of man. Revelation 13:8 reminds us that Jesus, the Lamb of God, was slain before the foundation of the world. We need to know that Adam and Eve did not catch God by surprise when they fell from temptation into sin. Before they were ever created, the Lamb of God had already been slain. In the mind of God, justice had already been served. The situation was already taken care of.

Isaiah Chapter 53, in verses 7-12, prophetically declares:

He was oppressed, and he was afflicted, yet he opened not his mouth: he is brought as a lamb to the slaughter, and as a sheep before her shearers is dumb, so he openeth not his mouth.

He was taken from prison and from judgment: and who shall declare his generation? For he was cut off out of the land of the living: for the transgression of my people was he stricken.

And he made his grave with the wicked, and with the rich in his death; because he had done no violence, neither was any deceit in his mouth.

Yet it pleased the LORD to bruise him; he hath put him to grief: when thou shalt make his soul an offering for sin, he shall see his seed, he shall prolong his days, and the pleasure of the LORD shall prosper in his hand.

He shall see of the travail of his soul, and shall be satisfied: by his knowledge shall my righteous servant justify many; for he shall bear their iniquities. Therefore will I divide him a portion with the great, and he shall divide the spoil with the strong; because he hath poured out his soul unto death: and he was numbered with the transgressors; and he bare the sin of many, and made intercession for the transgressors.

God planned that Jesus would be the sacrificial lamb, the scapegoat for us. He would be the One who knew no sin, and would become sin. Mind you, there's a difference between the Old Testament scapegoat and Jesus. In the Old Testament, our sin was simply covered over, and man could have only temporary relief for the soul. But Jesus, the New Testament scapegoat, became one in spirit with sin, so that we could become one in spirit with righteousness. Our sins are *not* just covered over. They've been removed—obliterated.

Notice that Isaiah 53:12 doesn't say, "He died for the sins of many." It says He died for "the *sin* of many." Jesus didn't become sin, the action. He became sin, the nature. I used to look at that scripture and think, "Jesus, who knew no sins became sins that I might become . . ." Then I realized there was no "s" at the end of the word "sin." I'd wonder, "Just what sin did Jesus become?" Probably a *bad* one, since He had to become unrighteous as a result of it! So I tried to imagine just which bad sin He committed. But we know that the Bible says in 2 Corinthians 5:21, "He who knew no sin became sin." He became the very nature of sin that I could become the very nature of righteousness, so I could become His very own nature, and become absolutely one with God. ❀

PART IV

◆ ◆ ◆

Made Perfect in Christ

"And you are complete in him, who is the head of all principality and power."

— Colossians 2:10 —
The King James Bible

PUTTING ON RIGHTEOUSNESS

When Jesus Christ was raised from the dead, resurrection life was in Him. The Spirit of Righteousness rose Him up from the dead. That's when Jesus became a conqueror over sin. He became a conqueror over the devil. Jesus became the victor over every thing and every area that we needed victory in. And, by virtue of me being in Christ, I too became victorious. The very same Spirit of Righteousness that raised Christ from the dead dwells in me. *"O, that I might know Him and the power of His resurrection,"* says Philippians 3:10. The power of the resurrection of Jesus *is* the Spirit of Righteousness. We need to know Jesus and we need to know the Spirit of Righteousness.

Whenever you read about Joshua in the Old Testament, it's likely that you're reading a prophecy concerning the Messiah. Joshua is a representation of Jesus. Their names are connected: in Hebrew, Joshua is Y'hoshua, and Jesus is Yeshua. Both names mean "salvation." Joshua's life speaks of a time when the Savior would come, and what would be happening in the spirit in that day. A look at Joshua foretells the time when Jesus would be changed from unrighteousness to righteousness. In Zechariah, the third chapter, the Word of God says:

> *And he shewed me Joshua the high priest standing before the angel of the LORD, and Satan standing at his right hand to resist him. And the LORD said unto Satan, The LORD rebuke thee, O Satan; even the LORD that hath chosen Jerusalem rebuke thee: is not this a brand plucked out of the fire?*
>
> *Now Joshua was clothed with filthy garments, and stood before the angel.*
>
> *And he answered and spake unto those that stood before him, saying, Take away the filthy garments from him. And unto him he said, Behold, I have caused thine iniquity to pass from thee, and I will clothe thee with change of raiment.*
>
> *And I said, Let them set a fair mitre upon his head. So they set a fair mitre upon his head, and clothed him with garments. And the angel of the LORD stood by. And the angel of the LORD protested unto Joshua, saying,*

Thus saith the Lord *of hosts; If thou wilt walk in my ways, and if thou wilt keep my charge, then thou shalt also judge my house, and shalt also keep my courts, and I will give thee places to walk among these that stand by.*

Hear now, O Joshua the high priest, thou, and thy fellows that sit before thee: for they are men wondered at: for, behold, I will bring forth my servant the Branch. *Hear now, O Joshua the high priest, thou, and thy fellows that sit before thee: for they are men wondered at: for, behold, I will bring forth my servant the* Branch.

For behold the stone that I have laid before Joshua; upon one stone shall be seven eyes: behold, I will engrave the graving thereof, saith the Lord *of hosts, and I will remove the iniquity of that land in one day.* —Zechariah 3:1-9

He says in verse 9, *"And I will remove the iniquity and guilt of this land in a single day."* Isn't that precisely what happened when Jesus came into the presence of the Father after He had become one with our sins? When He came into the presence of the Father, the Father said, "The work is complete. Take the filthy rags of unrighteousness off of Him. Replace the filthy clothes of sin and deception, and put on new clothes. Clothe Him in righteousness." Furthermore, He said, "And in these clothes, You will stand and be the leader of My people."

The day that Jesus became our sacrifice was the day a new and righteous nature could be available to each and every one of us. No longer would we be enslaved by the nature of sin. God is not as interested in the *action* of sin as we had thought He was. Without a doubt, the action of sin hurts us. That's why God doesn't condone sin. But the action of sin does not produce the nature of sin, and that is very important to know as we consider the question of eternal life. I am righteous. I may falter and sin, but that does not put me back into the kingdom of darkness, or make me unrighteous all over again. It does not make Satan my father as he was before. It just shows that I'm ignorant. I'm not walking in the light that I've been given. More proof that if I had a better understanding of my recreated nature, I wouldn't be sinning!

The concentration of much of Christianity has been centered on all the "do's-and-don'ts." It seems that we would rather have people *looking* right and *doing* the right thing than to actually *be* right. We've preached Christian morality to the world. Perhaps we should have been preaching Christ instead! We say, "If you'll stop doing drugs, if you'll stop having abortions, if you'll stop committing adultery, if you'll stop being homosexuals, then God will be pleased with you." Not true. God is not pleased with righteous actions only. He's pleased with righteousness, and that only comes by faith in Jesus. As we've said, this faith will produce righteous good works. But the truth is, those right actions are meant to bless us—not to please God. Good works are for *our* benefit, not for His!

The Bible tells us that Jesus, referred to as Joshua, put on new clothes—"rich apparel," as it's called in Zechariah 3:5. According to the Word of God, He wears the breastplate of righteousness (Isaiah 59:17). Ephesians Chapter 6 tells us that we also are to wear the breastplate of righteousness because, "Out of our hearts flow the issues of life," (from Proverbs 4:23). Our life is contained in our hearts. The real you, the real me, is found in our hearts. And He says, "This is what I want protecting your heart—righteousness. So you'll understand that you're okay; that you've been made right; that you posses the very nature of God living inside you." Knowing that will protect your heart!

Here's what will break your heart—If you don't understand righteousness, and somebody comes along and tells you, "The reason you're not right with God is because you don't pray enough," or, "You're not spending enough time reading the Word," or, "You're not witnessing enough," or whatever. There's always something you can be convinced that you're not doing enough of! Without a doubt, praying, reading the Word, witnessing, are wonderful things to do. There's a blessing in them! But it's not what makes you right with God. Righteousness is your heart's best protection. Knowing that you are righteous will remind you that good works are what you *desire* to do—not what you *have* to do!

Conversely, I have to tell you that I just *love* when people stand up to testify, saying, "You know why things are going so good for me? Because I've been *witnessing*. Because I've been *giving*. Because I've been *praying.*" Well, we're so proud! But that's not the real reason that things are going so well for people. Things go good in our lives because *"Blessed be the God and Father of our Lord Jesus Christ, who hath blessed us with all spiritual blessings in heavenly places in Christ,"* (Ephesians 1:3). We're blessed because Jesus has done it all! Did I say, "Don't witness. Don't read your Bible. Don't pray?" Not at all—I'm saying that all Christian service must come out of the spirit; out of a heart of righteousness. We're not *trying* to be righteous by doing these good works of service. You see, when I know that I am unconditionally loved in a relationship, when I know that a person views me very highly, I have no problem responding accordingly.

AWAKE UNTO RIGHTEOUSNESS

Thank God for the New Testament! Grace overcame the law. Jesus fulfilled the law and moved it out of our way, so we would not have a consciousness of sin. The Old Testament people of God had a high degree of sin-consciousness. Their sin was ever before them. How much more, then, should we experience *freedom* from the consciousness of sin in the New Testament!

I'd say most every day of my life I have a real consciousness of my righteousness. I have an awareness that I'm under the grace of God. I feel God's pleasure, I feel the love of God. But, every now and then, something will happen that'll disturb my thinking.

Something might happen to make me think, "Hey, I really *am* a lousy person. I really *am* the very kind of person that so-and-so says I am." Thank kind of thinking, without exception, makes me feel like I'm absolutely nothing. It makes me feel like I can't do what I'm called to do. That why God doesn't want us to have any consciousness of sin.

What if I asked you to tell me something you do that you feel guilty about? Almost all of us could give a list of, "Well, sometimes I . . ." and, "Oh, yeah, I . . ." There's always something! But God wants us to be free from any sense of guilt. He wants us to be like Paul. Paul said, "I have offended no man," (2 Corinthians 7:2). He even went so far as to say, "I judge not my own self," (1 Corinthians 4:3). And these quotes come from a man who had persecuted Christians, even unto death. If I was the relative of one of the believers killed as a result of the persecutions of Paul (Saul), I think I might be offended! But Paul walked in the reality of righteousness. So should we! He lived like he preached—"*Therefore if any man be in Christ, he is a new creature: old things are passed away; behold, all things are become new.*" —2 Corinthians 5:17

That word "behold" means "to look, to see, and to hear". God wants you to look, and to see, and to hear all the fresh and the new that has come to you as a recreated man. Not the old. That's why Paul says, "Here's some wisdom for you—this one thing I know. Forget what lies behind, and press on towards the mark of the high call of God," (from Philippians 3:13-14). Here's a simple truth regarding vision. There's no way I can look backward and forward at the same time. My eyes must focus one or the other. God's Word tells me to focus on the fresh and the new that has come. He wants us to think on that which is good and lovely and of good report. He told us to renew our minds to the things of God. Don't "review" your minds back to who you were, or think about all the bad things in the past. God is blessed when we us focus on the fresh and the new, because that's what will bless us.

"That the communication of thy faith may become effectual by the acknowledging of every good thing which is in you in Christ Jesus," So says the book of Philemon, verse 6. Faith seems as though it is weak when we start acknowledging all the problems that are within us. "I always get angry," "I always act like a jerk," "I'm always broke" or "I'm never happy." That kind of thinking leads nowhere! That's how faith is rendered ineffective.

We've read the books, seen the television broadcasts, and heard the sermons of too many "faith weakeners." The church as a whole is full of people that want to remind us of all the things that we still need to do. But right now, let's allow Jesus to remind us that He's done everything. When He sat down at the right hand of the Father, He demonstrated that His redemptive work was finished. But *we* are seated at the right hand of the Father beside Jesus! That's because as far as redemption goes, my work is complete also. I can sit down, ceasing from any and all human endeavors to make myself righteous and pleasing to God. All I need to do is receive, to renew my mind. And as I acknowledge every good thing that is within me, my faith becomes effectual and I acknowledge that I've been made whole, and that the very power of God lives in me. I acknowledge that rivers of living water live with me.

"He that believeth on me, as the scripture hath said, out of his belly shall flow rivers of living water," says John 7:38. That's the same term used when the Bible talks about the river of life that is for the healing of nations, and the river of life that makes the city of God glad. I acknowledge that the fullness of the Godhead is in me. The power of the Spirit of God is in me (the Spirit of might), with the ability to do anything God has called me to do. The anointing abides within me.

We pray, "Oh Father, please give me Your anointing." *It abides within you.* "Oops—a baby is crying in church. There goes the anointing!" "Somebody's eyes weren't closed during the altar call? There goes the anointing!" No, the anointing abides within you. Sometimes, we allow outward situations to distract us. But the anointing isn't nervous, or planning on going anywhere. It abides within us. We must acknowledge every good thing that God has placed within us. When we do so, our faith becomes effectual.

Acknowledging our righteousness will build-up our confidence. It'll cause us to feel like we're "okay" before God. The best thing I can think of having in a relationship is a confidence that I can't ruin it or blow it. I want to feel that the relationship is going to be strong, no matter what I say or do. I want to feel that, no matter what, the commitment is strong enough for the relationship to continue on and keep growing. Does that cause me to say and do wrong things, just to put the relationship to the test? No, it doesn't. It causes me to want to be better and better! God wants us to be confident in our relationship with Him. When He says, *"I will never leave thee or forsake thee,"* in Hebrews 13:5, He means it. When He says, *"They shall call His name Emmanuel, which being interpreted is, God with us,"* in Matthew 1:23, He means He'll be with us. When Jesus said, *"Lo, I am with you always, even unto the end of the world,"* in Matthew 28:20, He means always. When Jesus gives the promise of the Holy Spirit, *"For He (the Spirit of Truth) dwelleth with you and shall be in you,"* —John 14:17, He means forever!

We were old wineskin's, like the ones described in Matthew 9:17. It says He could not put new wine (His presence) into old wineskin's because they would burst. He could have left us the way we were, but so great was His desire to share fellowship with mankind that He had to recreate us. He made us new wineskin's, new creations. When He did that, He was able to put the fullness of His Spirit in us. He made us brand new—just so we could contain all of Him. Colossians 2:9-10 says, *"For in Him dwelleth all the fullness of the Godhead bodily. And ye are complete in him, which is the head of all principality and power."*

Jesus didn't *do* any sins—He *became* sin so that we could *be-*

come the righteousness of God in Christ." The day I woke up to the fact that I was righteous was the very day I stopped having trouble with my sinful thoughts. I began to realize the extent that God has gone to in order to give me a righteous nature, and I became convinced that the nature of righteousness was stronger than sin. Just like light is more powerful than darkness, God is far above *any* principality or power. The power of righteousness is stronger than any sin in your life.

Paul said in Romans 3:25 and 26, *"Whom God hath set forth to be a propitiation through faith in his blood, to declare his righteousness for the remission of sins that are past, through the forbearance of God; To declare, I say, at this time his righteousness: that he might be just, and the justifier of him which believeth in Jesus."* Jesus has become the propitiation, or the mercy seat. The mercy seat was where God would meet with man. It's where God would cover the sins of His people. But now that Jesus has become the mercy seat, God doesn't cover sins. He removes them!

As we grow in Christ, there are things that were formerly a temptation to us, which are no longer a temptation at all. But I want to tell you how to stop *anything* that's not of God from being a temptation—by awakening unto who you are—by awakening unto righteousness. Consider the slave who discovers that he's been set free. Immediately he realizes, "I don't have to do what this tyrant master tells me to do." Before we came into the kingdom of God, we were under the control of the tyrant master, Satan.

But now we know that he is nothing but a powerless ghost, never to return to rule our lives.

Isaiah says that God has appointed righteousness to be our taskmaster. *"I will also make thy officers peace, and thine exactors righteousness,"* (Isaiah 60:17b). He has appointed righteousness to rule over us. My taskmaster, the righteous nature of God, is at work. It tells me, "This isn't the thing to do," or, "No, this is how God would handle that situation." Deferring to His leadership becomes very natural to me.

RIGHTEOUSNESS AND JUDGMENT DAY

There is nothing about us that God is angry at. Jesus has become the Mercy Seat, and every bit of God's wrath concerning us has been poured out on Jesus. There is nothing in your life that God is disappointed in. "But Claudia, you don't know what I do," you say. Perhaps *you're* disappointed in you, but God's not disappointed in you! You need to realize that God knew there would be areas in your life that would be a struggle to you, yet He still calls you to be confident in Him. He's confident in His ability, and He's confident in *your* ability to trust *Him*.

"Blessed is the man to whom the Lord will not impute sin," (Romans 4:8). Allow me to bring something to your remembrance—it has got to be one of the most unscriptural and ridiculous things

that we hear. Too bad we hear it so often! I was watching TV the other day, and they were saying that when we get to Heaven, there's video that's going to be played on a big screen TV, right in front of God and everybody, showing all the things we've done wrong. Even the things you did when you thought no one was looking! Have you ever heard something like that before? Of course you have. For future reference, let's call it the "big screen in heaven" doctrine. I don't have chapter-and-verse to verify this doctrine, but it sure can be effective in shaming us out of sin—for a little while, at least!

It's very possible that there will be a video played on that day, but it'll show all the righteous things you did—even your righteous thoughts. The rest will be burned: *Every man's work shall be made manifest: for the day shall declare it, because it shall be revealed by fire; and the fire shall try every man's work of what sort it is. If any man's work abide which he hath built thereupon, he shall receive a reward. If any man's work shall be burned, he shall suffer loss: but he himself shall be saved; yet so as by fire.* —1 Corinthians 3:13-15

That's the mercy and grace of God at work. If you saw all the sins you committed when you were on the earth, you wouldn't be real happy, would you? It'd be pretty embarrassing, not something that would bring us the "joy unspeakable and full of glory" feeling we expect heaven to produce! It would bring sorrow and sadness. But according to God, sin is not held to our account. Once we have received Jesus Christ, our old nature of sin is gone.

Are you getting comfortable with the idea that righteousness refers to nature, not actions? Which is to say, we're righteous whether we're naughty or nice, or whether we feel righteous or not. We're righteous because God has made us righteous.

There existed a group in Galatia that tried to establish their own righteousness through observance of the law. They said, "Listen, we know we started out believing in God. We had faith and righteousness, but now here's what we need to do in order to be pleasing to God." They began to bring in all kinds of rules and regulations to follow. The rules and regulations began to be lord, instead of Jesus Christ. Paul writes something to the effect of, "Didn't you start off believing the Gospel? So why are you doing this on your own? Who has bewitched you?" Then he asked, "Why have you fallen from grace?"

In the church language of today, we say a person has "fallen from grace" if he commits adultery, or if he stops attending church. When you and I try to start establishing our own righteousness by how good we are, we truly have then "fallen from grace." When we depend on grace, when we depend on the very nature of God, we have power over anything. When we fall into sin, we don't necessarily fall from grace. We've just fallen from rational and intelligent thinking. We're acting in ignorance. A fall from grace happens when we depend on ourselves to be made right before God.

I can never depend on me to be right before God *without* Him. But I can always depend on Him to keep me on the right path. He's got his hook in our jaw. We may start getting pretty far out there, but God gently reels us in, keeping us going in that path. We can trust Him.

In my own Bible teaching ministry, I'd get to the point where I'd say, "Boy, I'm getting scared to preach a message that sounds so radically different than what I usually hear preached by others." But God would assure me that He would keep me from falling off the edge. He encourages me to keep going, even if it feels like I'm out on a limb. Now, more than ever, I'm not one of those ministers who are scared of saying the wrong thing. Hey, if I say the wrong thing, my heart is in the right place. God is so gracious that He'll cause you to hear the right thing! I never plan to, but if I say the wrong thing, God will watch over my words, like He watches over my heart.

And when we got born again, what most Christians don't understand, is they were born again unto a righteous nature. Our nature becomes just like God, Who is righteous, and that sets Him apart from any other creation in all the universe. God wanted a family so much; and when Adam fell, He could no longer have fellowship with Adam, and Adam could no longer have fellowship with Him. So God paid the extreme price, sending Christ Jesus to the death—even the extreme death of the cross. That was so you and I could have an exchange of natures, so that the unrighteous could become righteous through Jesus, who would become one with our sins so that we could become one with His nature. We need to understand that our nature is righteous. If we don't, we'll always be striving to somehow be right with God. We'll always be looking for a way to "Oh, if only I could do this, then . . ." But I want to tell you—it's now! We don't have to worry about that, because we believe in Christ Jesus and He's done it all. He's done everything for us.

MADE PERFECT IN CHRIST

Remarkable as this sounds, we're perfect in God's sight. Therefore, we should think of ourselves as being perfect. When Jesus walked the earth, many people regarded Him simply from a human point of view. They looked at Him and they said, "Ah, He's from Nazareth. He's Joseph's son and Mary's son. He's just Jesus." People made a mistake by regarding Him from a human point of view. When Jesus went to minister in the region He came from, few people received miracles because they thought wrongly of Him. Now, by faith, we no longer regard Jesus from a human standpoint. But at the same time, the Bible exhorts us not to regard anybody from a human point of view—not even ourselves! Don't look at yourself from a human standpoint, as mere man, nothing more. We've got to look at ourselves from God's point of view. We need to remember who we are spiritually. We're more than what we see in the mirror!

We acknowledge the promises of God, *"that the communication of thy faith may become effectual by the acknowledging of every good thing which is in you in Christ Jesus,"* (Philemon 1:6). That's how we become effectual in faith.

If you want to be weak in faith, just start acknowledging every bad, horrible thing that you can possibly think of about yourself. Go ahead and agree with a negative opinion of yourself, and it will weaken your faith. This is an absolute fact. Just start focusing in on your failures, on all of your problems, on all the areas that you don't feel fully developed in. Start focusing in on things like these, and I'll guarantee that soon you'll feel weak, like you can't do a thing.

The Bible tells us that when Moses led the children of Israel out of Egypt, they began to look back with homesick remembrance from whence they had come. In doing so, they found a constant opportunity to return. After they had left Egypt and experienced the wilderness, they forgot that they had been slaves, that they were beaten and abused. They chose to remember only things like, "Oh, the garlic was great. Wasn't the food wonderful?" Soon, they began to long for something that wasn't real.

You and I cannot look back and look forward at the same time. That's not possible. That's why Paul says, "Forget what lies behind." When we "fight the good fight of faith," the fight is for your identity in Christ Jesus. How many times has someone said to you, ". . . and you call yourself a Christian!" It's your identity in Jesus that is going to be attacked. If you don't hear it from others, you're likely to hear it from yourself unless you're watchful. Isn't it interesting that you can be told over and over again about how much of Jesus' nature is in you—and then one person comes up and says, "I didn't even *know* you were a Christian." And there it all goes! That one statement just bombards your mind. But God says, "I want you to bring down all the strongholds that would arise up against your knowledge of Jesus Christ." This is the nature of our warfare, the fight of faith.

When God talked to Peter in a vision, saying, "Bring down the sheet filled with clean and unclean animals. Now, kill and eat." Peter said, "No, Lord, I'll never do that. I'll never touch anything unclean." God said, "Peter—whatever I have proclaimed as clean, don't you defile by saying it's not clean." In that same way, God has proclaimed every one of us clean. We're not to defile anything, including ourselves, by letting our mouths agree with Satan by saying that we're not what God says we are.

"Effectual" means "active, operative, powerful." That word is used one other time in the New Testament. When the Bible says, "The Word of God is alive and full of power," that word is "effectual." The Word of God is effectual—it's alive, it's full of power. Think about what the Word of God does. You can be in a situation and speak the Word of God—and that Word has more power than anything else in all of creation.

I remember the story that Dena Smith, a minister we went to bible school with, tells about a terrifying situation she faced while ministering in Africa. While traveling on a highway with her husband and two children, her car broke down. After her husband went for help, some men broke into their van. One of the men, whose name meant "one who wields the knife well," told her that they were going to rape and kill her while her children watched. As he brings the knife up, she says, "No weapon that is formed against me shall prosper!" And he couldn't bring the knife down to stab her! Three times he tried, and three times she proclaimed, "No weapon that is formed against me shall prosper." Right then, headlights filled the rear window—her husband had returned with help. The men were never able to harm her at all, and later, they were caught. During the trial, one of the men said he did not know why he could not harm her. We know that he couldn't do it because the Word of God is powerful!

I remember when the power of that particular Word was birthed in Dena. Terry Mize, a Christian missionary, was a guest speaker at our bible college. Terry said, "You've got to get Scriptures inside you. Then, when you get scriptures *inside* you, you've got to let them come *out of* you." He then told a story about picking up a hitchhiker while ministering in Mexico. As they were driving along, the hitchhiker pointed a gun at him and said, "Get out of the car." Terry got out of the car, and the hitchhiker said,

"Take off your clothes." So Terry took off his clothes. The man said, "Give me your wedding ring." Terry took off his wedding ring. Then, the man said, "Now, I'm going to kill you." Terry looked at him and said, "No weapon that is formed against me shall prosper!" When Terry said that, the man cocked the gun, and shot six rounds at Terry from less than two feet in front of his face. Not one bullet hit him! Now, you've got to agree with me—that was a miracle from God! Like we said, the Word of God is alive and full of power. And that Word went deep inside of Dena when she heard it—ready to come out when the situation demanded its miracle power!

As righteous men and women of God, we need to learn how to activate our faith. We've spent far too much time trying to get something we already have. It would be like me spending all night and all wishing that I had dark hair. "Oh, God, please give me dark hair." That would be such a waste of time. Why? Because I already have dark hair! It's even more of a waste of time to try to get God to do things He's already done within us, to try and convince God to give us what He's already given us.

Specifically, it's a waste of time to say, "God, I just want to be righteous." If you believe in Jesus Christ as your Lord and Savior, *you are righteous!* "I just want to be righteous before you." *You are righteous.* "Father, I just want to be right with you." *You are right with Him.* When we acknowledge every good thing that is within us, our faith becomes alive and full of power. That's much more powerful than "trying to get faith." The Word of God in our hearts activates our faith.

My goal is that every one of us would grab hold of who we are in Christ, and that we'd step out in the power of that revelation. As pastors of our church, we love to see people become empowered by the Christ in them, then to go out and implant that knowledge inside other people. It's sad to see ministers that go out, not knowing "diddles" about what Jesus has done for them. All they can do is repeat the same message, over and over again. People need to hear a Gospel message that will help them to grow in Christ.

Romans 7:4 says, *"Wherefore, my brethren, ye also are become dead to the law by the body of Christ; that ye should be married to another, even to him who is raised from the dead, that we should bring forth fruit unto God."* We are "dead to the law, and are united to Christ." Let's acknowledge that truth. I want you to see yourself so unified with Jesus—not only on the inside but all around you—so close to you that He likens it unto a marriage. Totally unified, and acknowledging every good thing that is within me.

I've heard Romans 8:1 used in this context: "There's no condemnation as long as you're living after the Spirit, not after the flesh." That's not what this verse is talking about. It says, *"There is therefore now no condemnation to them which are in Christ Jesus, who walk not after the flesh, but after the Spirit."*

Paraphrased, it's says, "There is no condemnation for *you*,"—now here's the description of "you"—"who walks not after the flesh but after the Spirit." You're not walking after the flesh, are you? You're walking after the Spirit. The man of the flesh is someone who has never received Jesus. The flesh speaks of the unrenewed, Godless nature of man. The man of the Spirit refers to the person who has received Jesus and is recreated in His image. So He says, "There is therefore now no condemnation for you who are in Christ Jesus." You're not condemned in any way.

"Oh, but you don't know how I act," you say. The Word says you're not condemned in any way. "You don't what I've done!" You're still not condemned in any way. "You don't know how I am—just ask my wife; ask my husband." Maybe we should ask Jesus instead. He says, "You're complete, filled with My approval. You're perfected in Me. There is now no condemnation for you."

If you're under condemnation, you are not effectual in faith. You imagine that, "I have no right to say anything, I have no right to exercise authority in this situation." Somebody will come to you and say, "This person needs prayer, they need deliverance." And condemnation will cause you to reply, "You know, I'm not prayed up right now." I'll have you know that Jesus is prayed up *all* the time—and, by virtue of me being in Christ, I can rely on *Him*. It's not dependent on *me*; it's dependent on *Him*. He says, "I want you to get this on the inside of you—I love you so much, I've made you an heir of all things. I've not condemned you—I love you!"

Don't receive feelings of guilt anymore! There is therefore now no condemnation for those who are in Christ Jesus, who walk not after the flesh, but after the Spirit. I want you to acknowledge something on the inside of you and make the promises of God our own. Say, "I don't walk after the flesh." Say it out loud! "I walk after the Spirit and therefore there is no condemnation for me." Now, take a minute and let that truth soak into your mind. In Jesus, there's no condemnation. It's like you never have done anything wrong. Like you never *will* do anything wrong. That's how God sees it!

Let's take a look at another Bible verse. Romans 8:17 says, *"And if children, then heirs; heirs of God, and joint-heirs with Christ; if so be that we suffer with him, that we may be also glorified together."* We're fellow heirs with Christ. Everything that Christ *has* received from God, and *will* receive from God, is ours. We're joint heirs. One translation talks about us having joint seating with Christ, saying, "we are sharers of the throne of God." Think of yourself as having everything that Christ has. Is there anything that's not His? All things were made through Him and all things are for Him. He's the heir of everything, the heir of *all* things. By virtue of us being in Christ, we become heirs of all things along with Him.

We can only be effectual in faith when we feel *real good* about ourselves. And the only way for us to feel real good about ourselves is to seek out the opinion of God. You can be around people that feel real good about you one day. But maybe they'll feel real lousy about you the next day! If you depend on others for your self-esteem, you'll always be up and down. Don't get your self-esteem from any person. Not even from yourself, because your opinions can change, too. Get your self-esteem from God. He always loves you. He always sees you as good, righteous, pure, holy and perfect. You always have His favor.

God gives us the same favor He gives Jesus. He sees us as perfect in the same way He sees Jesus as perfect. Scripture says that Moses had favor with God, but we're different than Moses was when he walked the earth—we're righteous. We're different than Abraham was—Abraham had righteousness attributed to him, but we've been infused with righteousness. It is our very being, our very nature.

We're "consecrated," which means "set apart." We're purified. I Corinthians 1:2 says, *"Unto the church of God which is at Corinth, to them that are sanctified in Christ Jesus, called to be saints, with all that in every place call upon the name of Jesus Christ our Lord, both theirs and ours."* Think about purified water. Any dirt, bacteria, germs or impurities that used to be in it is gone. We're made holy in Christ, we're selected and called to be saints. We already are everything that God has called us to be. We're sanctified; we're set apart—by virtue of being in Christ Jesus.

In that same chapter, look at verse 30: *"But of him are ye in Christ Jesus, who of God is made unto us wisdom, and righteousness, and sanctification, and redemption."* Jesus gave us righteousness, conse-cration, and redemption. Because I'm in Christ, I'm righteous, I'm consecrated. I've been redeemed from the penalty of sin. I'll never—ever—stand before God with any charge against me. Counter to popular belief, we'll never stand before God and have to answer for all the bad things we did. We'll stand before God so that God can say, "Thank you for receiving my Son!"

Are you familiar with the term "pleading the blood?" You'll hear people say, "I plead the blood over my house, over my family, etc. . . ." People usually refer to it as a prayer of protection. But the way I understand pleading the blood is, when you stand before the court of heaven, and are asked, "How do you plead?" I plead the blood because it keeps us innocent in every way. When we stand before God, He'll acknowledge that we're His children.

Right now, as you finish reading this book, I'm putting out seed. I'm sowing righteousness. Your job is to take that seed and sow it to yourself. It will produce a harvest of blessings that will change your life, and the lives of the people around you. We'll have a long talk in heaven about the blessings that came into your life when you Awoke Unto Righteousness!

Made in the USA
San Bernardino, CA
21 September 2014